FOR THE GOOD OF THE CAUSE

By the Same Author:
CANCER WARD
THE FIRST CIRCLE
ONE DAY IN THE LIFE OF IVAN DENISOVICH
WE NEVER MAKE MISTAKES

For the Good of the Cause

Alexander Solzhenitsyn

Translated by David Floyd and Max Hayward
Introduction by David Floyd

WHITE LION PUBLISHERS LIMITED
London, New York, Sydney and Toronto

Copyright © Frederick A. Praeger Inc., 1964

First published in the United Kingdom
by Pall Mall Press, 1964

White Lion Edition, 1974

ISBN 0 7274 0031 2

Made and printed in
Great Britain
for White Lion Publishers Limited
138 Park Lane, London W1Y 3DD
by
R. Kingshott & Co. Ltd.,
Deadbrook Lane, Aldershot, Hampshire

TRANSLATORS' NOTE

As in all translations of Soviet works, the chief
difficulty encountered in this rendering of Alexander
Solzhenitsyn's *For the Good of the Cause* is the termi-
nology of an unfamiliar social and political system.
The translators have not burdened the reader with
outlandish terms, but it would be well to bear in mind
that Grachikov, as head of the Town Committee (*gor-
kom*), is subordinate in the Party hierarchy to the
Secretary of the District Committee (*obkom*). The
school with which the story deals is a technical school
which students enter at the age of fourteen or fifteen,
after their first seven years of general education. The
main emphasis here is on practical work rather than on
theory.

The translators have appended extensive extracts
from the public controversy which this work by Alexander Solzhenitsyn has aroused in the Soviet Union.
Since the polemic has now run its full course, this
record of a literary debate gives readers an excellent
introduction to Soviet literary politics.

INTRODUCTION

Alexander Solzhenitsyn first became known to readers both inside the Soviet Union and outside it as a writer of considerable talent through his short novel *One Day in the Life of Ivan Denisovich*. It appeared in Russian in the Soviet literary journal *Novy Mir* in November, 1962, and in English translation in Britain and America in the spring of 1963. *One Day* was followed by two short stories, *An Incident at Krechetovka Station* and *Matryona's Home*, published by *Novy Mir* in January, 1963. *For the Good of the Cause* is Solzhenitsyn's latest published writing and appeared in *Novy Mir* in July, 1963. The editors of that journal have promised to publish further works from his pen in the course of 1964.

Literary creation and publication in the conditions prevailing in Russia today are inevitably as much political acts as purely literary achievements. Some account of the literary and political background of Solzhenitsyn's emergence as a writer may thus contribute to an appreciation of his work. And, since the official reaction to *For the Good of the Cause* has been far more political than literary, we have translated the principal reviews published in the Soviet press, and these appear as an appendix to this volume. In this way we hope not only to acquaint readers with an important piece of contemporary Russian writing, but also to enable them to appreciate what the publication of such a work means in Russia today and how it is handled by Soviet critics. I believe that Solzhenitsyn's story and the reactions to it provide a remarkable insight into the nature of Soviet society today and, incidentally, throw light on the attitudes of the "liberal" and "Stalinist" camps.

The zigzag course followed by Soviet policy, both domestic and foreign, since the death of Stalin in 1953 has been due primarily to the operation of two contradictory forces. On the one hand, Stalin's successors have been keenly aware of the need to rid the country, especially its administration and economy, of the dead hand of Stalinist bureaucracy. This is a constant and very pressing concern, dictated by the need for revitalizing all aspects of Soviet life and putting some drive into the sluggish state machine. On the other hand, the Soviet leaders have a deeply rooted fear of the implications of any general and genuine liberalization of thought and culture. They have recognized and abandoned the evils of extreme authoritarianism without having embraced true democratic freedom. Their real aim is in fact an impossibility: a society under the complete, centralized control of a single party, but bursting with enterprise and enthusiasm in every field and at all levels. In the field of culture they demand great and powerful works of art from an intelligentsia deprived of the necessary freedom of creation and subject to every kind of pettifogging interference. In other words, the men who rule Russia want to rid their country of the worst, most inefficient, and unpopular type of Stalinist official, without at the same time offering any encouragement to the liberal ambitions of the intellectuals.

It is this permanent and by its nature insoluble conflict of interests that compels the leaders to go first this way and then the other, or even sometimes in two directions at once. From time to time, Khrushchev feels the need to send a galvanizing shock through the whole system and so rid it of some of its dead weight. But each administration of the shock treatment is almost invariably followed by a panicky recoil from the possible consequences.

By far the biggest shock of this kind was the one administered by Mr. Khrushchev in his "secret" speech to the Twentieth Congress of the Soviet Communist Party, in February, 1956. This, the first major act of "de-Stalinization," naturally gave rise to a burst of "liberal" enthusiasm among Soviet intellectuals. Though this was quickly damped down, writers and intellectuals in general nevertheless continued to exploit the denunciation of Stalin to their own advantage and to loosen the Party's grip on them. By the end of 1961, they were enjoying what was, by Soviet standards, a considerable measure of freedom.

At the end of 1961, at the Twenty-second Congress of the Party, Khrushchev delivered his second major anti-Stalin shock. On this occasion, he made further damning criticisms of the men such as Molotov who had been most closely associated with Stalin. The Congress ended with the dramatic removal of Stalin's remains from the mausoleum on Red Square. This highly symbolic act once again raised hopes among the liberal-minded intellectuals. But their hopes were shattered almost immediately by the guardians of Russia's "ideological purity" at a conference in November, 1961. The intellectuals had to wait another year, until the appearance of Solzhenitsyn's *One Day*. Publication of this powerful story of life in the concentration camps of Stalin's day was said to have taken place on Khrushchev's instructions and was clearly intended as a further move in de-Stalinization.

But again the hopes of the liberals were dashed. The decision to publish *One Day* unfortunately was made at a time when Khrushchev was under fire because of the failure of his Cuban adventure and when the reactionary elements in the Party were struggling desperately to regain their lead. In December they seized on Khrushchev's discomfiture to stage what was certainly a deliberate provocation against the "liberals." They arranged for Khrushchev to be shown an exhibition of abstract art in Moscow, to which he reacted, as he was no doubt intended to, with violent and scabrous comments on liberalism and the intellectuals. Having thus, in their turn, administered a blow to the liberals, the Party ideologists succeeded at two meetings—one in December, 1962, and the other in March, 1963—in re-establishing the principle of rigid Party control over literature and the arts. At the same time, the Stalinists managed to consolidate their hold over every important organization and journal connected with the arts, except for the Moscow branch of the Union of Soviet Writers and *Novy Mir*. Khrushchev appeared to have surrendered completely to the reactionaries.

Though reduced to silence, the liberals were far from routed. Nor had Khrushchev succumbed to the reactionaries in the Party. Toward the end of April, 1963, he seemed to have recovered from his Cuban setback and to have made himself undisputed master of the internal situation once more. As a result, the meeting of the Party's Central Committee summoned in June to lay down the line on ideological matters marked a clear return to the middle-of-the-road policy preferred by Khrushchev. This turn for the better was evidenced by the resumed publication of Ilya Ehrenburg's highly nonconformist memoirs in *Novy Mir* and by the appearance in *Izvestia* of *Tyorkin in the Other World*, a mordant anti-Stalinist satire by *Novy* .

Mir's editor, Alexander Tvardovsky. A balance of forces seemed to have been established between Stalinists and liberals.

It was at this point that Tvardovsky, the shrewdest and most dogged of the liberal spokesmen, found it opportune to publish a new work by Solzhenitsyn: *For the Good of the Cause.* The issue of *Novy Mir* containing this story was sent to the printer on June 31 and finally passed for publication on July 19. It was an unmistakably political gesture, which was intended to carry the battle against Stalinist officialdom yet a step further.

Post-Stalin literature has by now seen many other works critical of contemporary Soviet society. But none has depicted with such supreme literary skill the gulf between the ordinary, "little" people and the officials whose whole mentality and conduct are firmly set in a "Stalinist" mold. In *One Day*, Solzhenitsyn had condemned Stalinism primarily with reference to the past. But now he provided a very precise picture, drawn in sharp, clear strokes, of the "little Stalins" who are still so powerful in the everyday life of the Soviet Union. Solzhenitsyn deliberately leaves the reader with the impression that the little Stalins are firmly entrenched in Soviet society and are indeed typical of the ruling bureaucratic apparatus. This bald statement has caused considerable uneasiness in Party circles and has drawn the fire of hostile critics, who accuse Solzhenitsyn of distorting Soviet reality.

It is for the reader to judge the literary quality of the story, which in a brief compass gives an extraordinary cross-section of Soviet life, and Solzhenitsyn succeeds in conveying its very essence. He runs the whole gamut, from ordinary students, workers, and teachers to the omnipotent officials in Moscow, terrifying in their faceless, Kafkaesque anonymity. In between is the hierarchy of local officialdom—Knorozov, the Stalinist boss of the District Party Committee; Khabalygin, the self-seeking director of the local relay plant; Grachikov, the "liberal" Secretary of the local Party organization, who is, however, helpless to counteract Knorozov's influence.

In August, 1963, a month after publication of the story, the defenders of Party bureaucracy launched their first attack in the *Literary Gazette** with an article entitled "What Is 'Right'?" It was written by Yuri Barabash, associate editor of the paper and a man of apparent authority among the literary bureaucracy.

Barabash's article was mainly a political commentary on the picture and characters drawn by Solzhenitsyn. Barabash found himself obliged to acknowledge Solzhenitsyn's ability as a writer and spoke of his "great and honest quality" and his "unique sensitivity to any manifestation of evil or untruth or injustice." But then he went on to dismiss his work as a "failure,"

* *Literaturnaya Gazeta.*

on the grounds that the situation could not occur in real life. The little Stalins described by Solzhenitsyn were already figures of the past, said Barabash, and the new men who had come forward to replace them were by no means the helpless characters typified by Grachikov.

Barabash's article indicated Party disapproval of Solzhenitsyn's story. In the past such an article would have been followed by others in the same vein, and ultimately by a *mea culpa* on the part of the author. But in 1963, things were different, and there were no further comments in the *Literary Gazette* for several weeks. Indeed, the only other important blow to be struck by the Stalinists was a bad-tempered comment in the September issue of their principal journal, *Oktyabr*. In this, the reviewer was mainly concerned with ridiculing Solzhenitsyn's "idealistic concept of good and evil" and his division of Soviet society into "saints" and "devils."

Then, surprisingly enough, the *Literary Gazette* of October 15 printed a vigorous reply to Barabash by a well-known novelist, Dmitri Granin. Like Barabash, Granin avoided purely literary criticism and discussed only the rights and wrongs of the issue raised in Solzhenitsyn's work. He concluded that the story was a serious and courageous attempt to grapple with the question of what the "good of the cause" was, and rejected Barabash's charge that Solzhenitsyn had been untrue to life.

But a few days later the *Gazette* published a further article, this time from the pen of a certain R. N. Seliverstov, an official of the Communist Party in Leningrad whose work brought him into regular contact with many educational establishments of the kind described by Solzhenitsyn. He was, presumably, a carefully selected mouthpiece of the Party *apparat*. The main burden of his criticism was that, though Solzhenitsyn's condemnation of the little Stalins was effective, it was irrelevant, because such characters belonged to the past. Solzhenitsyn was behind the times.

More important, however, than Seliverstov's article was the statement by the editors of the *Literary Gazette* which accompanied it, a statement well worth careful study for the light it throws on the official Soviet view of literary creation. The editors admitted the value of an "exchange of opinions"; they were even prepared to accept the existence of people like Solzhenitsyn's villains. What they objected to was his failure to commit himself to a clear-cut Party point of view on the issues his story raised. It was obvious that what they really disapproved of was Solzhenitsyn's stark realism, or "critical realism," in the words of a high Party official whom the editors quoted. The Party can accept realism, but not unadulterated realism. It always has to be mixed with a good measure of optimism to make it palatable. In short, it is one thing to depict and denounce little Stalins, but another thing to give the impression that they are still all-powerful.

None of this criticism was particularly damaging from Solzhenitsyn's point of view or that of his readers, nor was it powerful or concerted enough to put an end to debate.

It was left to Tvardovsky and *Novy Mir* to show the contempt with which such attacks could now be treated. In the October, 1963, issue (which, however, did not go on sale until December), Tvardovsky published three carefully chosen contributions, all approving strongly of *For the Good of the Cause*. With his clever exploitation of this material, Tvardovsky revealed his thorough command of the techniques of Soviet political controversy.

The first contribution was a letter from three "old Communists," one of whom—Yampolskaya—was, conveniently, a former associate of Lenin's. Couched in delightfully ingenuous and unintellectual terms, the letter simply said flatly that Solzhenitsyn had done a good job and that Barabash had tried to mislead his readers. The telling quality of such a letter in present-day Soviet conditions can be understood only if it is realized that it has become *de rigueur* for the Party to solicit the support of "old Leninists" on all possible occasions. There is no higher "political authority" today.

The second contribution was a straightforward

demolition of Barabash's arguments by an obscure but hard-hitting literary critic. He placed Barabash clearly on the side of the Stalinists and appealed for support for an author of Solzhenitsyn's great talent.

Finally, there was a letter from two Leningrad workers who took sides with Solzhenitsyn and supported his pillorying of the Stalinist bureaucrats. Here, too, the argument itself was less important than the social status of the writers. The *Literary Gazette* had produced an "ordinary reader" in support of its views. Tvardovsky went one better and produced two genuine, real-life workers, to whose "authority" lip-service has to be paid in a proletarian society.

Thus Tvardovsky has in fact shown that he can outplay the Stalinists at their own game. If they could find people to say that Solzhenitsyn's treatment of his theme is "abstract" and out-of-date, Tvardovsky could find as many or more who would affirm that, on the contrary, it was true to life. Furthermore, if anyone cared to discuss the rights and wrongs of the incident depicted by Solzhenitsyn and the characters of men like Knorozov, that was just what the liberals wanted.

What matters is that *For the Good of the Cause* has been published, that no one could force its withdrawal or alteration, and that it was left to the readers to decide whether or not it was a good story and a true one.

DAVID FLOYD

FOR THE GOOD OF THE CAUSE

1

"Fayina, who's got the schedule for the electrical classes?"

"What do you want it for if you've got radio?"

"Please reduce the noise here by about twenty decibels. . . . There's a new comrade here—I want it for him."

"I'm sorry. What subject are you going to be giving here?"

"Generators . . . and power-transmission theory."

"There's so much noise, you can't hear a thing! And they call themselves teachers! . . . The schedule is over there in the corner. Go have a look."

"Susanna! How are you?"

"Lidia, my dear! How well you look! Where did you spend the summer?"

"A good question. I spent all of July on the building site!"

"On the building site? But didn't you have a vacation?"

"Not really. Three weeks instead of eight. But I didn't really mind. *You* look a bit pale to me."

"Grigori! What have you got down for the electricians? You mean you've scheduled only two days?"

"But none of the other departments have fixed their classes past September second. It's all provisional. Comrades—who's that leaving? Comrades! Listen! Quiet! I repeat—Fyodor Mikheyevich asked you not to go away."

"But where is he?"

"In the new building. He'll be right back. Then we can talk about the business of moving."

"Well, it better be settled soon. We've already got out-of-town students coming in. Do we have to find them places to live or will the dormitory be ready?"

"God knows! It's dragged on so long. Why on earth can't we ever get anything done on time?"

"I'm getting two rooms in the new building, Maria Diomidovna, and that'll do me fine! Electrical engineering in one and measurements in the other."

"So am I. I've got one room for electronics and another for insulating materials and lighting."

"Well, I'm really glad, for your sake. What you have now isn't a laboratory. It's a dumping-ground for broken glass."

"All this stuff lying around in crates in the corridor and the cellar—it's a nightmare! But with the shelves we've put up in the new building there'll be a place for

4

everything: ignitrons, thyratrons, and what have you. It'll be great."

"Vitali, stop smoking! If you want to smoke you should ask the ladies."

"Let me introduce our new engineering teacher, Anatoli Germanovich. This is Susanna Samoilovna. She is head of our mathematics department."

"Don't be funny. What do you mean, head of the department?"

"Well, head of the examination board, then. Isn't that the same thing? Except you don't get paid for it. Oh, and you must meet someone else—Lidia Georgievna. She's one of the most important people around here."

"Important! I'm probably the least important. As a matter of fact, before you know it *you'll* be more important."

"I bet you only say that because I'm wearing glasses."

"No. Because you're an engineer and a specialist. But they could easily do without me. I'm quite superfluous."

"What do you teach?"

"Russian language. And literature."

"You can tell from Lidia Georgievna's smile that she doesn't feel at all superfluous. In the first place, she's in charge of our youth organization."

"Really? Did the students elect you?"

"No, the Party Buro assigned me to the Komsomol *
Committee."

"Come on now, Lidia, no false modesty. The kids
asked for *you* and nobody else. And they've done it
now for four years in a row."

"I'll go further than that. I'd say that Lidia Georgievna deserves most of the credit for getting the new
building put up."

"You're making fun of me."

"I don't quite understand. Who built this new building of yours? Was it the Trust† or did you do it yourselves?"

"We did it together. But that's a long story."

"Let's hear it, Lidia. We've got nothing else to do
while we're waiting."

"Well, it was like this. The Trust told us it didn't
have enough money this year for all its jobs and it
would take another couple of years to get ours done.
So we asked: Can we help? And they said: Okay. If
you do, you can have the building by the first of September. We jumped at the chance. We called a general
meeting of the Komsomol . . ."

"But where could you hold a meeting here?"

"Well, we managed in the corridors and on the

---

* The Communist Youth League.

† An organization uniting several economic enterprises in the
same area and engaged in the same work—in this case, building.

6

stairs, and we had loudspeakers in the classrooms. That was the best we could do. Anyway, we got a meeting together and put the question to them. And the answer was: Yes. So we split up into work groups. At first we put a teacher in charge of each group. But the boys said that wasn't necessary—they could manage on their own. We were worried about the fourteen- and fifteen-year-olds, though. We were afraid one of them might get caught under a crane or fall or something. But we kept an eye on them."

"Wasn't it chaos?"

"We did our best to make it work. The foreman in charge told us a week ahead how many hands he would need, what kind, and when. So we set up a sort of headquarters and decided who was to do what. The kids worked every day—some before classes and some after. And a lot of them worked on Sundays too. They decided that everybody should put in at least two weeks' work during the summer vacation. Of course we tried to fix it so that out-of-town students could do their share either at the start or the end of the summer. But even if they were needed in the middle they showed up."

"Amazing!"

"Not at all. What *was* amazing was that it was all done without any kind of pressure. You wouldn't have recognized those kids. The people from the Trust just

7

couldn't believe it. They said: We can't keep up with them, we just can't."

"Incredible."

"You don't believe me? Ask anybody you like."

"It's not that I don't believe you. I suppose enthusiasm is natural, and a good thing too. But the trouble is that in this country the word has become hackneyed. It's abused all the time—take the radio, for instance. What *I* hear constantly at the factory is: 'What's in it for me? What does the job pay? Let's have it in writing.' And nobody raises an eyebrow—'incentives' and all that."

"And that's not all. They took a copy of the architect's plan and made a scale model of it. Then they carried it at the head of the May Day parade."

"Lidia Georgievna is giving you the romantic side. But to really understand it you have to hear the practical side. This school's been in existence for seven years and all this time we've been stuck out here near the railroad. A while ago they added a one-story wing for workshops and gave us another small building about half a mile from here, but even that didn't help much. And then Fyodor Mikheyevich managed to get hold of some land right in town where we could build. There were some shacks on it that had to be pulled down first."

"That didn't take long, did it?"

"No. They dug two holes with power shovels and put in the foundations for the school building and the dormitory. They got as far as building one story and then everything came to a stop. For the next three years there was never any money. During all those changes in Moscow we were always overlooked—whether they split up the ministries or amalgamated them, we were always ignored. And the snow and rain didn't help either. But now they've set up these economic councils* and the one we come under gave us some money on the first of June last year, and . . ."

"Dusya, open the window. These men! They really filled the room with smoke!"

"Do we have to go outside every time we want to smoke?"

"Well, that's not what the teachers' room is for."

"What jobs did *you* do on the building site?"

"Oh, all sorts of things, like digging the ditches for the boiler room."

"As a matter of fact, we dug *all* the ditches. For the electric mains, and . . . *And* we filled them all in again."

"And unloaded bricks from the trucks and stacked

---

* The organizations created by Khrushchev for local economic planning as a reaction to the excessive centralization under Stalin.

them in the hoist. And we cleared the earth out of the foundations."

"And we removed all the trash, brought up all the stuff for the central heating and the flooring, and then we did a lot of cleaning up and scrubbing."

"So actually the builders only had to send skilled men, no laborers?"

"As a matter of fact, we even trained some of the boys and girls to do skilled jobs. We had two teams of learners: plasterers and painters. They were really good at it. It was a pleasure watching them."

"Where's that singing coming from? Outside?"

> *We're sick and tired of darkness and gloom*
> *We'll put TV in every room*
> *With diodes, triodes, and tetrodes, too*
> *We'll make bigger and better tubes for you!*

"Without even looking I can tell that it's one of the third-year classes."

"They're good, aren't they? I'd like to get a look at them. Can we see them from the window?"

"Come over here. Marianna Kazimirovna, could you just move your chair a little?"

". . . Don't you believe it! The latest fashion is the 'barrel' line. Haven't you seen it? It's fitted in the waist, then it widens, then it narrows again, and then tapers down to mid-calf. . . ."

". . . I know another lake a little further away. You ought to see the carp I've caught there!"

"Lidia, watch where you're going. There are people sitting here."

"Here we are, Anatoli Germanovich. Just lean out. See that bunch of boys and girls?"

In airplanes, sputniks, and everywhere
Our vacuum tubes have found their place
Here on earth and up in space
Electronics sets the pace!

"They sure are enthusiastic. You can see they really mean it."

"They're so proud of that song: 'The Electronics Anthem.' They wrote it themselves and they do it so well. They even won the second prize in a local contest. Look! Only the girls are singing. The boys just stood there like this in the contest too, but they do come in on the chorus at the top of their voices."

"I'll tell you why I'm watching them like this. You see, I'm rather nervous because I'm used to teaching grownups. I once gave a lecture—'The Progress of Science and Technology'—at my son's school, and I nearly died of embarrassment. No matter what I did, I couldn't get them to pay attention. The principal pounded the table, but not even he could make them listen. My son told me afterward that they locked the cloakroom and nobody was allowed to go home. He said they often do that when there are visiting delegations or special events. So, to get even, the kids just keep talking."

"But you can't compare that with a technical school. Things are quite different here. We don't have any of those types with more money than brains who are just passing their time. And the principal here has greater powers because of scholarships and dormitory places. . . . Though actually we've never had a dormitory in our seven years and they have to get private accommodations."

"Does the school pay for them?"

"The school gives them thirty rubles each—that's the standard rate and it's supposed to be enough. But a bed costs a hundred rubles a month—a hundred and fifty for something a little better. So some of them rent one bed for two. And they live like that for years. Of course they're fed up. . . . You seemed a bit skeptical about our enthusiasm. There's nothing to be skeptical about. We are just tired of living badly. We want to live well! Isn't that why people did voluntary work on Sundays in Lenin's time?"

"True."

"Well, that's what we've been doing. . . . There they are. Look out the window."

. . . bigger and better tubes for you!

"How far is it from here into town?"
"About half a mile."
"But they still have to walk that half a mile. And a lot of them have to do it twice a day each way. And although it's summer and we haven't had any rain for three days, we're still knee-deep in mud. We just can't ever dress up. We have to wear boots all the time. Long after the streets in town are nice and dry we still get absolutely filthy."

. . . up in space

"So we had a meeting and talked things over: How much longer were we supposed to go on suffering? You should see the miserable little holes where we have classes. And there's no room for social activities. I think that's what bothers the students most of all."

. . . sets the pace!

"Lidia Georgievna! Ma'am!"
"Here I am!"

"We must see you. Can you spare a moment?"

"I'll be right there. . . . Excuse me."

". . . He really scored a great goal—with his back to the goal post and over the head, from the penalty line—right under the crossbar."

". . . This can't be your hat! That style went out ages ago. The hats they're wearing now look like flower pots upside down."

". . . Marianna Kazimirovna, can I bother you for a moment? . . ."

". . . I'm hoping to get part of the basement for a rifle range. I've already told the boys."

". . . I'm not leaving, Grigori Lavrentyevich. I'll be outside, on the stairs. . . ."

2

"Now who wanted to see me? Hello! How are you? It's so good to see all of you!"

"Congratulations, ma'am!"

"And congratulations to you." Lidia raised her hand and waved to them. "You've really earned it! Good for you and welcome back! In our new building!"

"Hooray!!!"

"Who's that over there trying so hard to keep out of my sight? Lina? You've cut your hair! Why? It was so lovely."

"Nobody wears long hair any more."

"The things you girls will do just to be in style."

Lidia, wearing a blue-green tailored suit and black blouse, looked neat and trim. She had a friendly, open face. Standing on the landing outside the teachers' room, she studied the young people crowding around her from the narrow passage and staircase. Usually there wasn't much light here, but on this sunny day there was enough to see the details of the students' clothes. There were scarves, kerchiefs, blouses, dresses, and cowboy shirts of every color and shade—white, yellow, pink, red, blue, green, and brown—dots and designs, stripes and checks, and plain solid colors.

The girls and the boys tried not to stand too close to each other. Pressed together in their own group, they rested their chins on the shoulders of those in front, craning their necks so as to see better. They all had happy, shining faces, and there was a buzz of excitement as they looked expectantly at Lidia.

She looked around and noticed that most of the girls had changed their hair styles during the summer. There were still a few who had old-fashioned braids tied with colored ribbons, and a few with simple center parts or not quite so simple curls brushed to one side. But most of them had those seemingly uncared-for, casual, untidy, but by no means artless hairdos, from pure blond to jet black. And the boys—the short and the tall, the fat and the thin—all wore gaudy, open-necked shirts. Some had their hair brushed forward, others wore it carefully brushed back or had crew cuts.

None of the very young students were here. But even the oldest were not yet beyond that tender, impressionable age at which the best in them could be brought out. Their faces mirrored that special eagerness.

The minute Lidia came out of the room, she was overwhelmed by those trusting eyes and smiles. It was the supreme reward of the teacher: students crowding around you eagerly like this.

They could not have said what it was they saw in her. It was just that, being young, they responded to everything genuine. You only had to take one look at her to know that she meant what she said. And they had gotten to know and like her even more during those months on the building site when she came, not dressed up, but in working clothes and a kerchief. She had never tried to order them around. She would never have asked anyone to do something she would not do herself. She had scrubbed, raked, and carried things together with the girls.

And although she was nearly thirty and married and had a two-year-old daughter, all the students called her Lidia, though not to her face, and the boys were only too proud to run errands for her. She always accompanied her instructions with a slight but commanding gesture, sometimes—and this was a sign of great trust —with a light tap on the shoulder.

"When are we going to move, Lidia Georgievna?"

"Yes, when?"

"Come now, we've waited so long, surely we can wait another twenty minutes. The principal will be back any minute."

"But why haven't we moved already?"

"Oh, a few little things still have to be done there. . . ."

17

"Always the same old story."

"We could put the finishing touches on ourselves if they'd just let us in."

A well-built youth from the Komsomol Committee in a red-and-brown checked shirt, the one who had called Lidia out of the teachers' room, said to her: "But we must discuss the details of the move. Who is going to be responsible for what?"

"Well, I thought of doing it like this . . ."

"Quiet, you guys!"

"My idea is to have a couple of trucks move the machinery and the heavy stuff. I'm sure we are quite capable of carrying the rest ourselves, like ants. After all, how far is it? . . . What do you think the distance is?"

"About a mile."

"It's fifteen hundred yards—I measured it."

"What did you measure it with?"

"With the gadget on my bike."

"Must we really have those trucks if it takes a week to get them? There are nine hundred of us. Couldn't we get all the stuff moved in a day ourselves?"

"Of *course* we can!"

"Sure!"

"Let's start right away. Then we can use this place as a dorm."

"The sooner the better, before we get rain."

"Now tell me, Igor"—Lidia tapped the young man in the red-and-brown shirt on the chest (like a general taking a medal from his pocket and firmly pinning it on a soldier)—"who's here from the Committee?"

"Practically everybody. Some of them are outside."

"All right, then. All of you get together right away, split up into groups, and make a list of them—but legibly, please! Put down the number of people in each group and decide who will take on which laboratories and which classrooms, depending on the weight of the equipment. And, as far as possible, organize yourselves by classes, but be sure that nobody takes on more than he can manage. When that's done, we'll show the plan to the principal, get it approved, and then put a teacher in charge of each group."

"Very good, ma'am," said Igor, standing at attention. "And this is the last time we'll have to meet in a corridor. Over there we'll have our own room. Hey, Committee members! Where should we meet?"

"Let's all go outside," Lidia proposed. "That way we'll see Fyodor Mikheyevich as soon as he gets back."

They made their way noisily down the stairs and out to the street, leaving the staircase empty.

Outside, on the lot in front of the school, with its scattered, stunted trees, another couple of hundred young people were waiting. The third-year students from the vacuum-tube department were still standing

around in a huddle, and the girls, arm in arm and looking at each other, were still singing:

. . . bigger and better tubes for you!

The younger ones were playing tag. Whenever
anyone was caught, they let him have it between the
shoulders.

"Why are you hitting me on the back like that?" a
plump little girl asked indignantly.

"Not on the back, on the backside!" retorted a
young man with a cap pulled down on his forehead
and a deflated volley ball tucked in his belt. But when
he saw Lidia Georgievna shaking a finger at him he
sniggered and ran off.

There were even younger students, just turned
fourteen, standing around in groups. They were neatly
dressed and rather shy, taking in everything very
carefully.

Some of the boys had brought their bicycles and
were giving the girls rides on the handlebars.

Fluffy white clouds looking like whipped cream
sailed across the sky. At times they hid the sun.

"As long as it doesn't rain," the girls said wistfully.

Three fourth-year students from the radio department—two girls and a boy—were talking together
in a separate group. The girls' blouses were of a simple,
striped material, but the boy's bright yellow shirt had

wild designs of palm trees, ships, and sailboats. Lidia was struck by this contrast, and something that had been puzzling her for a long time went through her mind. In her youth, her older brothers and the boys of her own age dressed rather simply, even drably; it was the girls who went in for bold colors and styles, as was only natural. But for some time now a great rivalry had been going on: Boys had begun to dress with greater care and even more gaudily and colorfully than girls, wearing loudly colored socks, as though it was not up to *them* to do the courting but to be courted. And the girls seemed to take them by the arm more often than they did the girls. Lidia was vaguely troubled by this odd behavior, because she feared that the boys were losing something of great importance to them.

"Well, Valery," she asked the young man in the yellow shirt with the sailboats, "do you think you got any wiser during the vacation?"

Valery smiled smugly: "Of course not! I got stupider."

"And doesn't that bother you? The girls won't think very much of you."

"Yes, they will!"

Judging by the expressions of the two girls, he had every reason for his self-confidence.

"What did you read during the summer?"

"Practically nothing, ma'am," Valery replied as

smugly as ever. He was not, it seemed, very eager to pursue the conversation.

"But why?" Lidia asked, rather put out. "Why did I waste my time teaching you?"

"Because it was in the syllabus, I guess," Valery shot back.

"If we read books, where would we find time for movies and TV?" the two girls burst in. "There's always something on TV."

Other fourth-year students gathered around.

Lidia frowned. Her thick, fair hair was pulled straight back, exposing her high forehead, on which both her disappointment and perplexity could be clearly seen.

"Of course, it's not for me, a teacher in a school where you learn about television sets, to try to turn you against TV. Watch it by all means, but not all the time! And besides, there's no comparison. . . . A show on TV isn't lasting. It's just for a day. . . ."

"But it's interesting and alive!" the young people insisted. "And then there's dancing . . ."

"And ski-jumping!"

"And motorcycling!"

"Books last for centuries!" Lidia said curtly but with a smile.

"Books last only one day, too," said a very serious young man. He was so round-shouldered he almost looked hunchbacked.

"Whatever gave you that idea?" Lidia asked indignantly.

"Just go to any bookstore," the round-shouldered boy said, "and you'll see how many novels are gathering dust in the windows. The shelves are piled high with them. Come back a year later, and they are still there. There's a bookstore on the block where I live and I know. After a while they pack them up and cart them away. A driver told me they are pulped and made into paper again. What was the point of printing them in the first place?"

In their second year, these boys had been her students. They had never said things like this. They had worked so well and gotten such good marks.

A discussion like this couldn't really be carried on while standing in a doorway amid all this commotion. But Lidia didn't want to drop it. That would have been a mistake.

"Well, you better have another look and see what *kind* of books are made into pulp!"

"I have looked, and I'll tell you if you like." The boy stood his ground. He wrinkled his forehead shrewdly. "Some of them were highly praised in the newspapers."

But the others were all talking at the same time, drowning out his voice. Anikin, the top student of his class—a husky fellow with a camera slung over his shoulder—pushed his way to the front. (They always listened to him.)

"Lidia Georgievna, let's be frank. At the beginning of the vacation you gave us a terribly long list of books, not one of them less than five hundred pages. How long does it take to read a book like that? Two months? And it's always an epic, a trilogy—'to be continued.' Who do they publish them for?"

"For the critics," came the answer.

"To make money."

"Maybe that's it," Anikin agreed. "Because technicians—and that's most of us in this country—must read technical literature and special journals to keep posted. Otherwise they'd get kicked out of their jobs, and rightly so."

"Right!" shouted the boys. "And when do we have time to read the sports magazines?"

"And what about movie magazines?"

"To my way of thinking," Anikin said impatiently, "authors who in this day and age write such long things really have a lot of nerve! We always have to find the most economical solutions when we design a circuit. When I sat in on the orals last year, the examiners kept on interrupting with questions like: 'Couldn't this be made shorter? Or simpler? Or cheaper?' Look at the sort of thing they write in the *Literary Gazette*. 'The characters,' they say, 'are too stereotyped and the plot is disjointed, but the ideas are just great!' That's like someone here saying: 'There's no current, the whole thing doesn't work, but the condensers are perfect.' Why don't they just say: 'This novel could have been one-tenth as long, and that one isn't worth reading.' "

"Well, I agree, some things could be shorter," Lidia said promptly.

The group of students surrounding her, which had steadily grown, howled with pleasure. That's what they liked about her: She never lied, and if she said she agreed, she meant it.

"But don't forget, books are a record of the people of our time, people like you and me, and about all the great things we have accomplished!"

"Memoirs are the thing nowadays," a boy with glasses and a funny-looking crew cut called out from the back. "Anyone who has reached the age of fifty or so goes and writes his memoirs—all about how he was born and got married. Any dope can write that kind of stuff."

"It all depends on *how* they are written," Lidia called back. "As long as they also write about the times they live in."

"But the kind of nonsense they put down," the boy said indignantly. " 'I caught a chill while strolling in the garden.' 'I came to the city and there were no rooms to be had in the hotel. . . .' "

The others pushed him aside and shut him up.

"About keeping things short, I'd like to say something." Another student raised his hand.

"I want to say something about the classics." Still another one raised his hand.

Lidia, seeing all their eager faces, smiled happily. She didn't care how excited they got or how they baited her. People who argue are open to persuasion. What she feared most of all in young people was indifference.

"Go ahead," she said to the first one, the one who wanted to speak about the need for precision in writing.

This was Chursanov, a boy with unruly hair, wearing a gray shirt with a turned and mended collar. His father was dead, and his mother, who worked as a caretaker, had other, younger children. That's why he had to quit regular school at fourteen and switch to a technical school. He hadn't been getting very good marks in Russian, but ever since he was little he had been putting together radio receivers. Here at the school they thought he was brilliant at it. He could find faulty connections without even looking at a diagram, as though he sensed them.

"Listen," Chursanov called out shrilly, "Anikin's right. Time is short. We can't afford to waste it. So what do I do? I just don't read novels and things at all."

They all roared with laughter.

"But you said you wanted to say something about keeping things short."

"So I do," Chursanov said in a tone of surprise. "When I'm at home, I turn on the radio. There's the news or a talk or something and at the same time I'm getting dressed or eating or fixing something. That's how I save time."

There was more laughter.

"What are you cackling about?" Chursanov asked, taken aback.

"There's really nothing to laugh about," Marta Pochtyonnykh came to his aid. She was a big, round-faced, rather plain-looking girl with thick black braids open at the ends. "Don't you agree, ma'am? It all depends on the book. It's all right if it tells you something you can't find anywhere else. But if all there's in it is something you can hear on the radio or read in the papers, then what's the point? Things are shorter and livelier in the newspapers."

"And they get things right. They don't make mistakes," somebody else called out.

"But what about the *way* things are said—the style?" a girl with a fresh complexion asked coyly.

"What do you mean, style? What's wrong with the style in the papers?"

"Lit-er-ary style, I mean," she answered, nodding her head at every syllable for emphasis.

"What do you mean by that?" Chursanov asked

with a puzzled look. "People falling in love and all that? Is that what you mean?"

"Of course style is important," Lidia said heatedly. She put her hand to her breast as though there was nothing of which she was more convinced. "You see, a book must go into the psychological aspect of things. . . ."

She was hemmed in by them on all sides, but not all of them could hear her, and they were talking and shouting to each other. Her face was flushed.

"You just wait!" she said, trying to calm the rebels. "I won't let you get away with it. We're going to have a big auditorium in the new building, so in September we'll have a debate." She gripped Anikin and Marta firmly by the shoulders. "I'll get all of you up on the platform, everybody who's had something to say today, and then . . ."

"Here he comes, here he comes!" The shout of the younger students was taken up by the older ones. One after the other, the young ones broke away, running faster and faster. The older ones got out of their way and turned to look after them. Teachers and students stuck their heads out of the second-story windows.

The school's battered pick-up truck, lurching, bumping, and splashing mud, was approaching from the direction of the town. The principal and his driver could be seen through the windshield of the cab being pitched from side to side. The students who had been the first to rush forward noticed that, for some reason or other, the principal looked anything but happy.

And their shouting ceased.

They ran alongside the truck until it came to a stop. Fyodor Mikheyevich, a short, stocky man in a plain, worn blue suit, bareheaded, with graying hair, climbed down from the cab and looked around. He had to get to the doorway, but his way was blocked by the young people crowding in on him from both sides, watching and waiting. Some of the more impatient ones started to ask questions:

"What's the news, sir?"

"When will it be?"

Then, louder, from the back of the crowd:

"Are we moving?"

"When do we move?"

Once again he looked over the dozens of expectant, questioning faces. It was obvious that he would not be able to put off answering them until he got upstairs. He'd have to do so right there and then. "When?" "When do we move?" The youngsters had been asking these questions all spring and summer. But at that time the principal and homeroom teachers had been able to brush off all such questions with a smile, saying: "It all depends on you. On how you work." But now Fyodor could do nothing but sigh and, not concealing his irritation, he said:

"We shall have to wait a little longer, Comrades. The builders haven't quite finished yet."

His voice always sounded a little hoarse, as though he had a cold.

A murmur was heard among the students. "More waiting." "Still not ready." "And the term begins the day after tomorrow, September first." "So now we'll have to go back to furnished rooms again."

The boy in the bright yellow shirt with the sailboats on it smirked and said to his girl friends:

"What did I tell you? Always the same old story. And mark my words, that's not the end of it."

They began to shout questions:

"But can't we finish it ourselves?"

The principal smiled and said:

"I see you want to do everything yourselves now! But I'm afraid that's not possible."

The girls standing in front tried hard to make him change his mind: "But, sir, can't we move in anyway? What still has to be done?"

The principal, a heavy-set man with a high forehead, looked at them in some embarrassment:

"Come now, girls, surely I don't have to give you all the details? . . . First of all, the floors are still not dry in spots. . . ."

"Then we won't walk on them! We'll put boards across them!"

"Then a lot of windows still don't have catches."

30

"That doesn't matter, it's still warm enough."

"The central heating hasn't been tested yet."

"That's nothing. That can wait till winter."

"Oh, and a lot of other little things. . . ."

Fyodor gestured helplessly. His forehead was a mass of wrinkles. How could he explain to them all the formalities involved in taking over the building? A deed of transfer had to be signed by the builders and by the other contracting party. The builder was ready to sign and hand over the building right away. And Fyodor was now so pressed for time that he too would have signed right away if only the school were the other contracting party. But this was impossible from a legal point of view, because the school had no one competent to make the required survey. Therefore the building office of the local relay factory had placed the contract on the school's behalf. The plant was in no hurry to sign for the building before it was quite ready, especially since it meant infringing on the regulations. Khabalygin, the manager of the plant, had been promising Fyodor all summer long that he would sign for the building in August, come what may. But recently he had been saying: "Nothing doing, Comrades. We won't sign the deed before they've put in the last screw." And technically he was right.

The girls went on plaintively:

"Oh, we *do* so want to move. Our hearts are set on it so."

"*Why* are you so set on it?" Chursanov shouted at them. He was standing on slightly higher ground than the others. "Whatever happens we've got to put in a month on a kolkhoz. Who cares which building we go from—this one or the other?"

"Oh, yes, the kolkhoz!" They suddenly remembered. Working on the building site all summer they had forgotten about the farm work.

"We won't be going this year," Lidia called out from the back.

It was only now that the principal noticed her.

"Why aren't we going? Why not?" they asked her.

"You should read the local paper, my friends. Then you'd know why."

"I bet we'll go anyway."

The principal pushed his way through the crowd and moved toward the door. Lidia caught up with him on the stairway, which was just wide enough for two people.

"Fyodor Mikheyevich! But they *will* let us have it in September, won't they?"

"Yes, they will," he replied absently.

"We've worked out a wonderful plan for moving everything over between lunch on Saturday and Monday morning, so as not to interfere with school-work. We're going to split up into groups. The Committee is arranging it now."

"Very good," the principal nodded, lost in his own

thoughts. What worried him was that only a few trifling details remained to be done and that Khabalygin, who must have seen this two or three weeks ago, could easily have speeded things up and signed for the building. It almost looked as though Khabalygin was dragging his feet.

"On a quite different matter, Fyodor Mikheyevich: We've discussed the case of Yengalychev in the Committee. He has given us his word and we're prepared to answer for him. So please restore his stipend on September first." Lidia looked at him pleadingly.

"You're always sticking up for them, aren't you?" The principal shook his head and looked at her with his pale-blue eyes. "And what if he does it again?"

"No, no, he won't," she assured him. They had reached the top of the stairs and could see the other teachers and the school secretary.

"I hope you're right."

He went into his cramped office and sent for his assistant and the department heads. He just wanted their assurance that they were ready to start the new school year, come what may, and that they had already prepared everything without having to be told.

In all his years at the school, Fyodor had tried to run things to keep everything going with a minimum of intervention on his part. He had finished his studies before the war and couldn't possibly keep up with all the latest developments in his rapidly changing field or with the specialists working under him. He was a modest man without personal ambition, and he had his own ideas about leadership. His idea of a leader was a man who, instead of following his own whims, settled things fairly by bringing together people who trusted one another and could work together harmoniously.

Fayina, the school secretary, came into the office. Very independent, and no longer young, she was wearing a colored kerchief tied under her chin. Its loose ends trailed behind her like a pennant as she walked. She handed the principal a diploma that needed his signature and opened a bottle of India ink.

"What's this?" Fyodor asked blankly.

"Gomiozina's diploma. You remember . . . she couldn't take the exam because she was ill. . . ."

"Yes, of course."

He tried the pen and dipped it in the ink. Then he clasped his right wrist firmly in his left hand. And then he signed.

When he was wounded for the second time—that was in Transylvania—not only did his broken collarbone fail to heal properly, he also suffered severe shock. It had affected his hearing and his hands shook, so he always signed important papers in this manner.

3

An hour and a half later the crowd had gone. Those teachers who had to prepare experiments remained behind with their lab assistants. Students were thronging the school office to register their addresses. Lidia and the Committee members drew up their moving plan and got it approved by the principal and the department heads.

The principal was still sitting with the dean of students when Fayina, her kerchief flying, burst into the office and announced dramatically that two limousines were coming from the town, apparently heading for the school. The principal looked out of the window and saw that two cars—one blue-green, the other gray —were indeed approaching.

There could be no doubt about it. Some bigwigs coming to visit the school. He should really go down to meet them. But he wasn't expecting anybody important, so he stayed where he was—at the open window on the second floor.

Big, white clouds were swirling across the sky.

The cars drew up to the entrance and out stepped five men in fedoras—two of them in the kind of green ones worn by the higher-ups in this town, the three others in light-colored ones. Fyodor immediately recognized the first man. It was Vsevolod Khabalygin, manager of the relay factory and hence nominally the "proprietor" of the new school building. He was a real big shot. By comparison Fyodor was a nobody, but Khabalygin had always been friendly toward him. Twice that morning Fyodor had tried to reach Khabalygin on the phone. He wanted to ask him to relent and let his building office sign for the new school and draw up a list of the work still to be done, but on both occasions he had been told that Khabalygin was out.

Fyodor had a sudden thought. Turning to the dean, who was standing there as tall and thin as a rail, he said:

"Grisha, maybe it's a commission to speed things up. Wouldn't that be great?"

And he hurried out to meet the visitors. The stern, brisk dean, of whom the students were very much afraid, followed after him.

But Fyodor had only got as far as the first-floor landing when he saw the visitors coming up the stairs, one after the other. First came Khabalygin. He was a short man, still under sixty, but overweight. He had passed the 250-pound mark long ago, and he was suffering as a result. His hair was graying at the temples.

"Ah—good." He stretched out his hand approvingly toward the principal. And as he reached the landing, he turned and said: "This is a Comrade from our Ministry in Moscow."

The Comrade from the Ministry was a good deal younger than Khabalygin, but he was also putting on weight. He permitted Fyodor to hold the tips of three smooth, dainty fingers for a moment and then moved on.

Actually, for two years "our" Ministry had had nothing to do with the school, which now was under the local Economic Council.

"I tried to get you on the phone twice today," Fyodor said to Khabalygin with a smile of pleasure and reached out to take him by the arm. "I was going to ask you . . ."

"And here," Khabalygin went on, "is a Comrade from the Department of . . ." He mentioned the department by name, but in his confusion Fyodor didn't catch it.

The Comrade from the Department was young, well-built, good-looking, and very well-dressed.

"And this," Khabalygin continued, "is the Head of the Electronics Section from . . ." Khabalygin said where from, but while speaking he resumed climbing the stairs, so again Fyodor failed to catch the name.

The Head of the Electronics Section was a short, dark, polite man with a small black mustache.

And finally there was the Supervisor of the Industrial Department of the District Party Committee, whom Fyodor knew well. They exchanged greetings.

Not one of the five men was carrying anything.

The dean was standing stony-faced, straight as a soldier, next to the banister at the top of the landing. Some of them nodded to him; others didn't.

Khabalygin managed to hoist his hefty bulk to the top of the stairs. Nobody could have walked next to him or passed him on the narrow staircase. After reaching the top he stood still, puffing and blowing. But his expression, always animated and forceful, discouraged any inclination to sympathize with him for the way in which, every time he walked or made a movement, he had to battle his large body, on which the layers of unlovely fat had been skillfully camouflaged by his tailors.

"Shall we go into my office?" Fyodor asked when he reached the top.

"Oh no, there's no point in sitting around," Khabalygin objected. "You go ahead and show us what you've got here. What do you say, Comrades?"

The Comrade from the Department pushed back the sleeve of his foreign raincoat, looked at his watch, and said:

"Of course."

Fyodor Mikheyevich sighed. "Honestly, we just don't know where to turn. We have to hold classes in two shifts. There aren't enough places in the laboratories. Different types of experiments have to be carried out in the same room, so that we're always having to put one batch of instruments away to make room for another."

He looked from one to the other, speaking almost in a tone of apology.

"You do make it sound terrible," Khabalygin said, and started to shake with either coughing or laughter —it wasn't clear which. And the rolls of flabby fat hanging from his neck like an ox's dewlap also shook. "It's amazing how you've managed to stand it these seven years!"

Fyodor arched his fair, bushy eyebrows: "But we didn't have so many departments then! And there were fewer students!"

"Oh well, lead on. Let's take a look."

The principal nodded to the dean as a signal that everything should be opened up, and he started to show the visitors around. They followed him without bothering to take off their hats and coats.

They went into a large room with shelves all around the walls, all crammed with equipment. A teacher, a girl lab assistant in a blue smock, and a senior student— it was Chursanov, the boy with the patched collar— were setting up an experiment. The room faced south and was flooded with sunlight.

"Well," Khabalygin said brightly. "What's wrong with this? It's a beautiful room."

"But you must understand," Fyodor said with some annoyance, "that in this one room there are three laboratories, one on top of the other: theory of radio and aerials, transmitters, and receivers.

"Well, so what?" The Comrade from the Ministry turned his large, handsome head and said, also with some annoyance, "Do you think there's more space between the desks in our Ministry after the latest reorganization? On the contrary, there's less than ever."

"These subjects are very closely related, after all." Khabalygin, very pleased with himself at this idea, patted the principal on the shoulder. "Don't act the pauper, Comrade. You're not so badly off as all that!"

Fyodor threw him a puzzled look.

From time to time Khabalygin moved his lips and his fleshy jowls, as though he had just had a good meal but hadn't yet had time to remove bits of food stuck between his teeth.

"What are these things for?" The Comrade from the Department was standing before some strange-looking rubber boots with turned-down tops which looked big enough for a giant. He touched them with the sharply pointed toe of his shoe.

"Safety boots," the teacher said quietly.

"What?"

"Safety boots!" Chursanov shouted in the impudent tone of one who has nothing to lose.

"Oh yes, of course," the Comrade from the Department said and followed the others.

The Supervisor from the District Committee, who was the last to leave the room, asked Chursanov: "But what are they for?"

"For when you repair a transmitter," Chursanov replied.

Fyodor had meant to show them all the rooms, but the visitors passed some of them by and went into the lecture hall. On the walls there were charts of English verbs and various visual aids. Geometric models were piled high on the cabinet shelves.

The electronics expert counted the desks (there were thirteen) and, stroking his toothbrush mustache with two fingers, asked:

"How many do you have to a class? About thirty?"

"Yes, on the average . . ."

"That means you have less than three to a desk."

And they continued their tour.

In the small television workshop there were about ten sets of various makes, some brand-new and some partly dismantled, standing on the tables.

"Do they work? All of them?" the Comrade from the Department asked, nodding at the sets.

"Those that are supposed to work all right," a young, smartly dressed lab assistant said. He was wearing a sand-colored suit with some kind of badge in his lapel, and a loud tie.

Some instruction manuals were lying around on a table. The electronics expert glanced through them, reading out the titles to himself under his breath:

Tuning a Television Set by the Test Table; The Use of the Television Set as an Amplifier; The Structure of Visual Signals.

"You see, there are no shelves here, but you still manage," Khabalygin commented.

Fyodor grew more puzzled every minute and wondered what the commission was getting at.

"That's because everything is next door in the demonstration room. Show them, Volodya."

"So there's a demonstration room as well? You certainly are well off!"

The door leading into the demonstration room was unusually narrow, more like a closet door. The slim, dapper lab assistant went through it with ease. But when the Comrade from the Ministry tried to follow him, he realized at once that he couldn't make it. The others just poked their heads in, one after the other.

The demonstration room turned out to be a narrow corridor between two sets of shelves from floor to ceiling. With the sweeping gesture of a professional guide, the lab assistant pointed to the shelves and said:

"*This* belongs to the TV lab. *This* to the electricity lab. And *this* is the radio lab's."

Instruments with dials, and black, brown, and yellow boxes cluttered the shelves.

"And what's *that* doing there?" the Comrade from the Ministry asked, pointing to something.

He had noticed that the assistant had managed to keep a little wall space free of instruments, and to this he had affixed a colored pinup—the head and shoulders of a young woman. Without seeing the caption you couldn't tell whether she had been cut out of a Soviet or foreign magazine. But there she was—a beautiful, auburn-haired woman wearing a blouse with red embroidery. With her chin resting on her bare arms and her head tilted to one side, she eyed the young lab assistant and the more worldly-wise Comrade from the Ministry with a look that was anything but a call to duty.

"Well! You say you have no space," the Comrade sputtered, struggling around to get out again, "but just look at the sort of stuff you hang up around the place!"

And, with another quick glance at the lovely creature out of the corner of his eye, he walked away.

The news that some awful commission was around had already spread throughout the school. People kept peering out of doorways and poking their heads into the halls.

Lidia, walking along one of the corridors, bumped into the commission. She stood aside, flattened herself against the wall, and studied them anxiously. She couldn't hear what they were saying, but she could tell from the look on the principal's face that something was wrong.

Fyodor took the Supervisor from the District Committee by the arm and, holding him back a little, asked quietly:

"Tell me, who actually sent this commission? Why is nobody from the Economic Council with you?"

"Knorozov just told me to come along. I don't know what's going on myself."

Khabalygin, standing on the upper landing, cleared his throat, which made the rolls of sallow fat on his neck shake again, and lit a cigarette.

"That's that. I suppose the rest is much the same."

The Comrade from the Department looked at his watch and said: "It all seems pretty clear-cut."

The electronics expert stroked his mustache with two fingers and said nothing.

The Comrade from the Ministry asked: "How many other buildings are there beside this one?"

"Two, but . . ."

"Really?"

"Yes, but they are quite terrible. Only one story and thoroughly inconvenient. And they're so far apart from each other. Let's go and look at them."

"And there are workshops in them too?"

"But listen, you're aware of the sort of conditions we're working in, aren't you?" Fyodor threw off the restraint imposed on him by the demands of hospitality and by the exalted position of his visitors. He really was worried now: "For one thing, we've got no dormitory. That's what we were going to use this building for. The young people have to live in private rooms all over town where there's sometimes foul language and drunkenness. All our efforts to build their characters are defeated. Where can we do it, on the staircase here?"

"Oh, come now, come now," the members of the commission protested.

"Character-building depends on you, not on the premises," the young man from the Department said sternly.

"You can't blame anyone else for that," the District Committee Supervisor added.

"Yes, you really have no excuse," Khabalygin said, spreading his short arms.

Fyodor turned his head sharply and shrugged his shoulders, perhaps in response to this attack on him from all sides, or perhaps to put an end to this relentless interrogation. He could see that if he didn't ask directly he was never going to find out what this was all about. He knitted his bushy, fair brows.

"I'm sorry, but I'd very much like to know on whose authority you are acting and what exactly you are after."

The Comrade from the Ministry took off his hat and

wiped his forehead with a handkerchief. He looked even more impressive without a hat. He had a fine head of hair, although it was thinning in spots.

"Haven't you heard yet?" he asked in a tone of mild surprise. "Our Ministry and"—he nodded toward his colleague—"the Department have decided that a research institute of national importance should be set up in this town and accommodated in the buildings originally intended for your school. That's it, isn't it, Khabalygin?"

"Yes, that's it," Khabalygin agreed, nodding his head in its green fedora. "That's the way it is." He eyed the principal somewhat sympathetically and gave him a friendly pat on the shoulder. "I'm sure you can stick it out for another couple of years, and then they'll build you a new school—an even better one! That's how things go, my friend, so don't let it get you down. It can't be helped. It's all for the good of the cause!"

Not very tall to begin with, Fyodor now seemed to become even shorter. He looked stunned, as if he had been hit over the head.

"But how . . ." Fyodor said the first, but by no means the most important, thing that came to his mind. "We haven't even kept this place in good repair." When Fyodor was upset, his voice, always gruff, dropped even lower and became quite hoarse.

"Don't worry about that," Khabalygin said. "I bet you painted it last year."

46

The Comrade from the Department went down one step on the stairs.

There were so many things the principal wanted to tell them that he couldn't make up his mind *what* to say first.

"What have I got to do with your Ministry?" he protested hoarsely, while blocking the visitors' way. "We come under the local Economic Council. You need a Government order for a transfer of this sort."

"You're quite right." The commission members pushed him gently aside, making their way down the stairs. "We're just preparing the necessary papers. We expect the final okay in a couple of days."

The five men went down the stairs while the principal just stood there staring blankly after them.

"Fyodor Mikheyevich!" Lidia called out, coming down the corridor. For some reason or other, she had her hand clasped to her throat. Her blouse was open at the neck and one could see how sunburned she had gotten while working on the building site. "What did they have to say?"

"They are taking the building away from us," he replied in a flat, almost toneless voice, without raising his eyes.

And with that he went into his study.

"What?" she cried out after a moment. "The new one? They're taking it away from us?" She hurried after him, her heels tapping on the floor. In the doorway she bumped into the bookkeeper. She brushed her aside and rushed in after the principal.

Fyodor Mikheyevich was walking slowly toward his desk.

"Listen!" Lidia called out in a strained voice. "What is this? How can they do such a terrible thing? It's not right!" Her voice was becoming shriller with every word. She was saying out loud what *he* should have shouted at them. But he was the principal, not a woman. Tears were now streaming down her cheeks. "What are we going to tell the kids? That we've cheated them?"

He couldn't remember ever having seen her cry before. He slumped into his chair and stared vacantly ahead at his desk. His forehead was one mass of wrinkles.

The bookkeeper, an elderly, shriveled-up woman, her straggly hair gathered in a bun at the nape of her neck, was standing there holding a checkbook.

She had heard everything. She would have gone away at once and not bothered him, but she had just spoken to the bank and been told that she could cash a check. The check had already been made out, with the amount and date filled in. She therefore had to see the principal, in spite of everything. She put the long, blue-striped book down in front of him and held it flat with her hand.

Fyodor dipped his pen in the ink, grasped his right wrist with his left hand, and raised it to write his signature. But even clutched like this, his hands still shook. He tried to put his signature on the check. The pen started to make some marks, then dug into the paper and sputtered.

Fyodor looked up at the bookkeeper and smiled.

She bit her lip, took the checkbook away from him, and hurried out.

4

Everything had happened so suddenly, and the commission had breezed through with such supreme confidence and so rapidly, that Fyodor had not been able to find the words he wanted while they were there, and even after they had gone he was still unable to decide exactly what to do.

He phoned the Education Department of the Economic Council. All they did was listen to his story, voice their indignation, and promise to look into the matter. Another time that might have cheered him up. But now it didn't. He knew the commission hadn't come for a social visit.

He felt so ashamed. He didn't know how he could face the students or the teachers, or anybody else he had gotten to help with the new building on the understanding that it would be theirs. All the plans which for months, even years, he and his colleagues had been making for the new building were now completely ruined. He would gladly exchange his own living quarters for worse ones if only the new building were given to the school.

His mind went blank. He just didn't seem able to think clearly.

Without a word to anyone and without putting on his hat, he went out to try to collect his thoughts.

Leaving the building, he set off in the direction of the railroad. But he wasn't really thinking about where he was going, because in his mind he was turning over the dozens of vitally important things the school was losing along with the new building. The railroad barrier came down just as he got to the crossing. Fyodor stopped, although he could have slipped through under it. A long freight train appeared in the distance, eventually reached the crossing, and quickly clattered past down the incline. But Fyodor didn't really take any of this in. The barrier was raised and he continued on his way.

He was inside the gates of the new building before he realized where he actually was. His legs had taken him there of their own accord. The main entrance, on which all the glazing and painting were already finished, was locked. So Fyodor went through the grounds, which had been marked off and cleared by the students. There was plenty of land, and they had planned to turn it into athletic fields.

One of the builders' trucks stood in the yard, and the plumbers were noisily throwing brackets, piping, and other stuff into it. But Fyodor paid no attention to them.

He went into the building. It made him feel good to hear his footsteps echoing on the stone slabs of the wide lobby. Its two cloakrooms, one on each side, were big enough for a thousand people. The hat- and coat-racks of aluminum tubing shone brightly, and maybe it was this that made Fyodor ask himself a simple question which—because all this time he had been thinking about the school, not its new occupants —had not occurred to him until now: What on earth would the new institute do with such a building? For one thing, they'd probably dismantle these cloakrooms, because the institute wouldn't have even a hundred people. And what about the gymnasium with its wall ladders, rings, horizontal bars, nets, and wire-meshed windows? Was all that going to be pulled down and thrown out? What about the workshops with their specially built concrete foundations under each machine? And the electric wiring? And the whole layout of the building around the lecture halls? And the blackboards? And the main lecture hall, designed like an amphitheater? And the auditorium? And . . .

At that moment a couple of painters and carpenters walked by him with their tools on the way out of the building.

"Hey! Listen!" Fyodor called to them, pulling himself together. "Comrades!"

But they went on their way.

"Listen, fellows!"

They turned around toward him.

"Where are you off to? It's not quitting time yet."

"We're through," the younger of the carpenters said blithely. The older one continued glumly on his way. "You can stay here and have a smoke. We're off!"

"But where to?"

"We've been taken off this job. Orders from above."

"But how can they take you off it?"

"*How?* Don't you know? They just send us to another job. We've been told to get there right away."

And, knowing the little gray-haired principal to be easy-going, the carpenter came back, tapped him on the hand, and said: "Give us a cigarette, chief."

Fyodor offered him a crumpled pack.

"Where's the foreman of this job?"

"Oh, he's already left. He was the first one to get out."

"What did he say?"

"He said that this has nothing to do with us any more. Another outfit is taking over."

"But who's going to finish here?" Fyodor asked impatiently. "What's so funny? Can't you see how much there's still to be done?" He frowned and looked angry.

"Who cares!" the carpenter shouted, puffing away at his cigarette and hurrying after his comrades. "Don't you know how they handle these things? The

Trust will make up a list of what we didn't finish and get it signed when they hand this over, and everything'll be all right."

Fyodor watched as the carpenter walked away lightheartedly in his dirty overalls. And with him went the Economic Council, which had taken on this ill-fated project after three years of paralysis, and which had finished it, right down to the last coat of paint and the last pane of glass.

Although the Council was deserting him, the thought of the innumerable, utterly pointless alterations that would have to be made in the building fired Fyodor's will to resist. He knew that justice was on his side. He hurried across the hallway, his steps echoing on the hard floor.

The room with the only working telephone turned out to be locked, so Fyodor rushed outside. A wind had started to blow, stirring up the sand and scattering it around. The truck with the workers was just going through the gateway. The caretaker was standing next to the gates. Fyodor decided not to go back with him. He felt in his pocket for a coin and walked over to a phone booth.

He called Ivan Grachikov, the Secretary of the Town's Party Committee. A secretary told him that Grachikov was in conference. Fyodor gave his name and asked her to find out whether Grachikov would see him and when. In one hour, he was told.

Fyodor continued on his way. While walking, and later, outside Grachikov's office, his mind went over every room on every floor in the new building. He couldn't visualize a single place where the institute wouldn't have either to knock down a wall or put up a new one. So he jotted down what all that would cost in a notebook.

For Fyodor, Grachikov wasn't just the Secretary of the Party Committee. He was also a friend from the War. They had been in the same regiment, though they hadn't served together very long. Fyodor had been in charge of communications. Grachikov had come from a hospital, as a replacement for a battalion commander who had been killed. They discovered that they came from the same part of the country, and on quiet evenings they used to get together or talk on the phone occasionally and reminisce about places they both knew. Then a company commander in Grachikov's battalion was killed and, as is the practice, all openings were filled with officers from the staff, so Fyodor was assigned to command the company—temporarily. "Temporarily" turned out to be very brief indeed. Two days later he was wounded, and when he got out of the hospital he was sent to a different division.

As he sat there waiting, it occurred to him that unpleasant things always seemed to happen to him in the last days of August. It was on the twenty-ninth of

August—that was yesterday's date—that he was wounded for the first time. And when he was wounded again, in 1944, it was on the thirtieth of August. That was today's date.

Some people left Grachikov's office and Fyodor was called in.

"A terrible thing has happened, Ivan," Fyodor said in a flat, hoarse voice as soon as he walked into the room. "Just terrible."

He sat straight up on a chair (Grachikov had gotten rid of those armchairs into which people sank so deep that their chins barely reached the top of the desk) and began his story. Grachikov rested his head in the palm of his hand and listened.

Nature had given Ivan Grachikov rough-cast features: thick lips, a broad nose, and big ears. But, although he wore his black hair brushed to one side, which gave him a rather forbidding look, his whole appearance was so unmistakably Russian that no matter what foreign clothes or uniform you might put on him, you could never disguise the fact that he was a Russian born and bred.

"Honestly, Ivan," the principal said with feeling, "don't you think it's stupid? I don't mean just for the school, but from the point of view of the state, isn't it plain stupid?"

"Yes, it's stupid," Grachikov said promptly, without shifting in his chair.

"Look, I've jotted down how much all these alterations will come to. The whole building costs four million, right? Well, these changes are sure to cost at least one and a half million, if not two. Look . . ."

From his notebook he read out a list of the various jobs and their probable cost. He was becoming more and more convinced that he had an absolutely airtight case.

Grachikov remained quite still, listening and thinking. He had once told Fyodor that the great thing about this job, compared to the War, was that he no longer had to make decisions by himself and on the spur of the moment, leaving the question of whether they were right or wrong to be settled in the other world. Grachikov much preferred to decide things without rushing—giving himself time to think and letting others have a say. It went against his grain to bring discussions and conferences to an end by simply issuing orders. He tried to argue things out with the people he was dealing with, to get them to say "Yes, that's right" or else have them convince him that *he* was wrong. And even in the face of very stubborn opposition he never lost his restrained, friendly manner. But his way took time. Knorozov, the First Secretary of the District Committee, had been quick to seize on this particular weakness of Grachikov's, and in his laconic fashion that admitted of no argument had once hurled at him: "You're too soft for this job. You don't do things in the Soviet way!" But Grachikov had stood his ground: "What do you mean? On the contrary, I do things the way the Soviets are supposed to: by listening to what other people have to say."

Grachikov had been made Secretary of the Town Committee at the last conference of the local Party organization, following some remarkable achievements on the part of the factory where he was then Party secretary.

"Tell me, Ivan, have you heard anything about this research institute? Whose idea was it?"

"Yes, I've heard about it." Grachikov continued to rest his head in his palm. "There was talk about it back in the spring. Then it got held up."

"I see," Fyodor said in a chagrined tone. "If Khabalygin had signed for the building, we would have moved into it around the twentieth of August, and then they wouldn't have shifted us."

They both remained silent.

During this silence Fyodor began to feel that the firm ground on which he had been standing was slipping away from under him. The prospect of a million and a half rubles' worth of alterations hadn't exactly caused an earthquake. Grachikov hadn't grabbed both of his phones at once, nor had he jumped up and rushed out of the room.

"So what did you hear? Is it a very important institute?" Fyodor asked dejectedly.

Grachikov sighed: "Once you know that its address is a P.O. box number, you don't ask any questions. With us everything is important."

Fyodor sighed too.

"But, Ivan, what are we going to do? They are planning to get a Government decision, and once they do it'll be all over. We've only got a couple of days. There's no time to be lost."

Grachikov was thinking.

Fyodor turned to face him. He leaned on the desk, propping his head on his hands.

"Listen. What about sending a telegram to the Council of Ministers in Moscow? This is just the right moment, when they're talking so much about the need for contact between the schools and real life. . . . I'll sign it. I'm not afraid."

Grachikov studied him closely for a minute. Suddenly all the sternness vanished from his face, giving way to a friendly smile. He began to talk the way he liked to, in a sing-song voice, in long, well-rounded sentences which had a tone of genuine warmth.

"My dear Fyodor, how do you picture this being

59

'arrived at, this decision by the Government? Do you imagine the whole Council sitting at a long table, discussing what to do about your building? Do you think they've got nothing better to do? And then I suppose you think your telegram will be brought in at just the right moment. Is that what you believe? No! A Government decision means that one of these days a Deputy Prime Minister will see one of the Ministers. The Minister will have some papers with him to make his report and at some point he will say: 'This research institute, as you know, has top priority. It has been decided to locate it in this town, in which there happens to be a building it can use.' The Deputy Prime Minister will then ask: 'Whom was it built for?' And the Minister will reply: 'For a school. But the school has got rather decent premises for the time being. We sent a commission of experts down and the Comrades studied the matter on the spot.' Then, before giving his final okay, the Deputy Prime Minister will ask one more question: 'Does the District Committee have any objections?' Do you get this—the District Committee! Your telegram will be returned right to this place with a notation on it saying: 'Check facts.' " Grachikov pursed his thick lips. "You've got to know how these things work. In this case it's the District Committee that holds the power."

He laid his hand on the telephone but didn't lift the receiver.

"What I don't like about this business is that the District Committee Supervisor was with them and raised no objections. If Knorozov has already given his okay, then, my friend, you're in trouble. He never goes back on a decision."

Grachikov was a little scared of Victor Knorozov. But then, there was hardly anyone in the district who wasn't.

He lifted the receiver.

"Is that Konyevsky? This is Grachikov. Say, is Knorozov there? When will he be back? I see. . . . Well, if he *does* come back today, tell him I'd be most grateful if he would see me. . . . Even after I get home this evening. . . ."

He put the receiver down but continued toying with it on its rest. Then he turned his eyes from the telephone to Fyodor, who was now holding *his* head in his hands.

"You know, Fyodor," Grachikov said earnestly, "I'm very fond of technical schools. I really like them. In this country of ours they're always making such a fuss over the top scientists. They don't seem to think that anyone with anything less than an engineering degree has any education at all. But for us in industry it's the technicians who matter most of all. Yet technical schools get a raw deal—and not just yours alone. Take your place for example. You accept kids this high"—he held his hand at desk level, though Fyodor had never accepted anybody that young—"and in the space of four years you turn them into first-class specialists. I was there when your kids were taking their examinations in the spring, remember?"

"I remember." Fyodor nodded unhappily. Seated at his large desk, to which another covered with a green cloth stood at a right angle, Ivan Grachikov spoke with such warmth you might have thought that instead of an inkwell, pen-holder, calendar, paperweight, telephones, carafe, filing basket, and ashtray, the desks were covered with white tablecloths and delicacies, which the host was offering his guest, even urging him to take some home with him.

"There was a boy of about nineteen, maybe, who was wearing a tie for the first time in his life, with a jacket that didn't match his pants—or is that the fashion now? He hung his diagrams on the board and set up on the table some regulator or calibrator or whatever you call it that he had made himself. This thingamajig clicked and flashed while the young fellow walked around waving his pointer at the diagrams and talking away like nobody's business—I was really envious. The words he used and the things he knew: what was wrong with existing indicators, the principle on which his thing worked, the power of the anode current, the meter readings, economic efficiency, coefficients and goodness knows what else! And he was only a kid! I sat there and I felt sorry for myself. After all, I thought, I've been around for fifty years, and what's *my* specialty? That I once knew how to work a lathe? But the sort of lathe I operated is a thing of the past. That I know the history of the Party and Marxist dialectics? But that's something everybody ought to know. There's nothing special about it. It's high time that every Party official should have some special knowledge or skill. It was boys like him who were running things in my factory when I was Party secretary. Who was I to tell them to increase productivity? I had to learn the ropes as best I could by keeping my eyes and ears open. But if I were a little younger, Fyodor, I'd enroll in your evening classes right away. . . ."

And seeing that Fyodor was now thoroughly depressed, he added with a laugh: "In the old building, of course!"

But Fyodor couldn't manage even a smile. He drew his head in, hunched his shoulders, and just sat there with a dazed look.

At this point a secretary came in to remind Grachikov that there were other people waiting for him.

5

Nobody had told the students what was going on. Yet by the next day they already knew all about it.

In the morning the sky was overcast and there was rain in the air.

Those who turned up at the school gathered in groups outside, though it was pretty cold. They were not allowed into the lecture rooms because the students on duty were cleaning them, and the labs were out of the question because apparatus was being set up there. So, as usual, they hung around the stairway in a crowd.

There was a hum of conversation. The girls were moaning and groaning. Everybody was talking about the building, the dormitory, and the furnished rooms. Mishka Zimin, a very strong boy who had broken all records digging ditches at the site, hollered at the top of his voice: "So we put in all that work for nothing, eh? For nothing at all! Well, Igor, how're you going to explain this one?"

Igor, one of the Committee members, was the dark-haired boy in the red-and-brown checked shirt who had drawn up the list of people for moving the

labs. He stood on the top landing looking rather sheep-
ish.

"You'll see, it'll all be straightened out."

"But *who's* going to straighten it out?"

"Well, *we* will. . . . Maybe we'll write a letter to
someone or something."

"That's a good idea," said a prim and serious-looking
girl with hair parted in the center. "Let's send a protest
to Moscow! They'll surely listen to us."

She was the meekest of them all, but now even she
had had enough and was thinking of quitting. She just
couldn't go on paying seventy rubles a month out of
her stipend for a bed.

"All right—let's get going!" another one cried, and
slapped the banister with her hand. She was an attrac-
tive girl, with jet-black, fine, curly hair, and was wearing a loose jacket. "I'm sure everybody will sign—all
nine hundred of us."

"That's right!"

"Sure!"

"You better find out first whether we're allowed to
collect signatures like that," somebody cautioned.

Valka Rogozkin, the school's leading athlete, the
best runner in the 100 and 400 meters, the best jumper,
and the loudest talker, was poised on the banister of
the staircase. He kept one foot on the stair, but he had
swung over the rail and was lying face downward on
it. His hands were interlocked on top of the rail and his

chin was resting on them. From this awkward position, ignoring the girls' outcries, he stared up at Igor. Valka Guguyev, a swarthy, broad-shouldered boy, sat recklessly in the curve of the banister, apparently unconcerned about the 20-foot drop behind him.

"Hey, wait a minute!" cried Valka Rogozkin in a shrill voice. "That's no good. I've got a better idea. Let's all stay away tomorrow, every single one of us."

"That's it—let's all go to the stadium," others backed him up.

"Where are you going to get permission?" Igor asked uneasily.

"Who says we've got to have permission?" Rogozkin burst out. "Of course they won't give us permission! We'll just stay away! Don't worry!" His shouts grew louder as he got carried away by his own words. "In a few days there'll be another commission. This one will come by plane and they'll give us our building back and maybe even something else besides!"

But some of them got worried.

"You're sure they won't stop our stipends?"

"They wouldn't do that to us!"

"But they might expel us!"

"That's not the way we do things," Igor shouted above the noise. "Just forget about it."

Because of all the racket they hadn't noticed old Dusya coming up the stairs carrying a pail. When she reached Rogozkin, she switched the pail from one hand to the other and raised the free one to give him a good smack on the backside with the flat of her hand. But he saw this just in time and hopped down from the banister, so that Dusya's hand only just brushed him.

"Now, Dusya," Rogozkin howled. And he wagged his finger at her in mock anger. "That's not the way *we* do things! Next time, I'll—"

"The next time you lie down like that," Dusya threatened him with the palm of her hand, "I'll teach you a lesson you won't forget in a hurry! That's not what banisters are for!"

They were all laughing loudly. Everybody at the school liked old Dusya because she was so down-to-earth.

She continued up the stairs, pushing past the students. Her face was wrinkled, but it was full of life, and she had a strong chin. She looked as though she deserved something better than this job.

"Aw, cut it out, Dusya!" Mishka Zimin blocked her way. "Why do *you* think they've given up the building?"

"Don't you know?" Dusya answered. "There's far too many parquet floors there. I'd go crazy trying to polish them."

And off she went, rattling her bucket.

There was another round of laughter.

"Hey, Valka! Do your stuff!" the boys on the top landing called to Guguyev as they caught sight of another bunch of girls coming into the building. "Lusya's coming!"

Valka Guguyev slipped off the banister, pushed the people next to him out of the way, and stood for a moment studying the rail. Then he gripped it firmly with both hands, swung his body up effortlessly, and calmly did a handstand over the steep drop.

It was a very dangerous stunt.

A hush fell over the staircase. All heads were turned toward him. The boys were impressed. The girls watched with a mixture of admiration and horror.

Lusya, the girl for whose benefit this was being done, was already on the staircase. She now turned and, her blue eyes wide open, looked straight up at Guguyev, who would have crashed right on top of her and on to the stone floor below if he were to fall. But he never did fall! Almost motionless, except for a slight swaying movement, he kept up his handstand over the stairwell and seemed in no hurry to come down. His back was to the drop, and his legs, held tightly together, arched out—on purpose, it seemed—right over the empty space. And his head, too, was strained back, so that he was looking straight down at tiny, slim Lusya, standing there wrapped in a light-colored raincoat with a turned-up collar. She was hatless, which suited her very well, and her short, fair hair was wet from the rain.

But could he really see her? Dark as the stairway

was, you could tell that the young hero's face and neck were purple from the rush of blood.

Suddenly the others called a warning:

"Look out!"

Guguyev immediately swung off the banister, landed lightly on his feet, and putting on an innocent look, leaned against the rail.

This performance could easily have cost him his stipend. It had happened to him once before when he rang the school bell ten minutes before the end of classes (so they wouldn't be late for the movies).

Before they'd had time to start their usual din again, Grigori Lavrentyevich, the gaunt and gloomy dean, started up the stairs. They made way for him respectfully.

He had heard that warning "Look out," and he realized there was something odd about the silence that met him. But he had not seen the cause of it all—particularly since Rogozkin, who never missed a chance to make trouble, immediately fastened onto him.

"Sir!" Rogozkin shouted down the stairs. "Why have we given up the building? After all, *we* built it!"

And he tilted his head to one side inquiringly and put on a halfwitted expression. From his very first day there, he'd played the fool and made people laugh, especially in class.

They all kept quiet, waiting to hear what the dean would say.

A teacher's life was like this—he was always having to answer such questions and you never knew what they were going to ask next.

The dean gave Rogozkin a long, hard look. But Rogozkin didn't flinch. He kept his head tilted to one side.

"Well, now," the dean said slowly, "when you finish school here . . . But wait a minute . . . how on earth *will* you finish school?"

"You mean because of athletics?" Rogozkin came back at him quickly. (Every spring and autumn he missed any number of classes because he was competing in either local or national events. But he always managed to make up for it and he never had bad marks.) "That's no way to talk. As a matter of fact," and he tapped his temple comically with a finger, "I already have some ideas up here about the project for my diploma."

"Really? That's fine. And when you finish school, where will you look for a job?"

"Wherever I'm needed most," Rogozkin answered with exaggerated gusto, throwing up his head high and standing at attention.

"Maybe you'll be given a job at the new building. Or perhaps some of the others will. So all that work you did on it will not have been in vain. It belongs to all of us."

"Oh, how nice! Nothing would please me more.

70

Thank you so much," Rogozkin said, brimming over with mock gratitude.

The dean went on his way. But before he had reached the corridor, Rogozkin reversed his decision in the same flippant manner:

"No, sir, I've changed my mind! I don't really think I want to work in that building!"

"Where do you want to go then?" The dean peered at him.

"I want to go and work on the virgin lands!" Rogozkin said loudly.

"Well, why don't you fill out an application?" the dean suggested with a faint smile.

And he went off down the corridor to the principal's study.

Fyodor himself was not there. He had not managed to get an appointment with Knorozov the day before, so he had gone down to the District Committee again today. But the teachers who were now waiting in the study for a call from the principal were not very hopeful.

A few drops of rain splashed against the windowpanes. The rough, uneven ground right up to the railroad was wet and dark.

The heads of departments were poring over the huge sheets of their schedules. They were passing colored pencils and erasers to each other and coordinating their classes. Yakov Ananyevich, the Secretary of the Party Buro, was sitting at a little table by the window near the safe with the files of the school's Party group and was sorting papers. Lidia was standing at the same window. In the way women have of changing their looks overnight, she had turned from the happy, brisk, youthful woman of yesterday into the middle-aged, haggard one of today. And she had changed yesterday's blue-green suit for a darker one.

The Party Secretary, short and balding, was dapper and clean-shaven, with a clear, fresh complexion. He was talking without interrupting his work. He handled the papers in their folders as delicately as though they were living things, taking great care not to crease them, and he treated documents written on thin paper with something akin to loving care.

His voice was soft and quiet, but you could hear every word.

"No, Comrades, certainly not. There will be no general meeting. Neither will there be any meetings on this subject by departments or by classes. It would mean giving the matter undue attention, and there's no point to it. They will find out all about it sooner or later, without us telling them."

"They already know," the dean said. "But they would like some explanation."

"Well, so what?" Yakov Ananyevich replied calmly, dismissing the problem. "You can explain things to them privately, and that's what you'll have to do. What you should say? What you should say is: This institute is of vital importance to the nation as a whole. It is concerned with the sort of thing we are studying. Today, electronics is the basis of all technical progress, and no one must be allowed to put any obstacles in its way. On the contrary, we must do everything we can to further it."

Nobody said anything. The Party Secretary carefully turned over two or three more papers, but he couldn't find the one he wanted.

"Actually, you don't even have to go into all that. You can just tell them that this is a State institute and the why's and wherefore's of the matter are none of our business."

He turned over some more papers and found what he wanted. Then he looked up again, turned his clear, calm eyes on them, and said:

"Hold meetings? Make this the subject for a sort of formal debate? No, that would be a political mistake. As a matter of fact, if the students or the Komsomol Committee insist on a meeting, then they must be dissuaded."

"I don't agree!" Lidia turned on him so abruptly that her short, brushed-back hair shook.

The Party Secretary looked at her blandly and asked in his usual punctilious manner:

"But what is there for you to disagree with, Lidia Georgievna?"

"First of all," and saying this she drew herself up and moved toward him, "first of all . . . well, it's your whole tone! It's not only that you're already reconciled to their taking our building away, but you even seem pleased—yes, actually *pleased!*"

The Party Secretary spread his hands slightly, without moving his arms.

"But, Lidia Georgievna, if the national interest is involved, how can I be anything *but* pleased?"

"It's your approach I don't like . . . I mean the principle of the thing!" She couldn't keep still any more and started pacing the small room, gesticulating as she spoke. "None of you has as much to do with the young people as I do. After all, I'm with the Komsomols from morning till night. And I know how it'll look to them, the thing you're trying to push down their throats. They'll think we're afraid to tell them the truth—and they'll be right! How will they ever respect us again? Eh? When something *good* happens we let everybody know about it. We plaster it all over the walls and talk about it on the radio. But when there's something *bad* or hard to explain, then they're supposed to find out as best they can and rely on rumor, eh? Is that what you want? It's all wrong!" Her voice rang out, but, unfortunately, for the second time

74

that day she found herself on the verge of tears. "No! You can't do this, especially not to young people! Lenin said that we should never be afraid to bring things into the open. Publicity is a healing sword, he said."

She choked with tears and left the study abruptly so as not to break down in front of everybody.

The Party Secretary watched her go with a pained expression on his face; shutting his eyes, he shook his head sadly.

Lidia went quickly down the dark corridor. Near the storeroom with its crates of vacuum tubes, two third-year students called out to her. While cleaning up, they had come across the scale model of the new building and wondered what to do with it. It was the model they had carried, hoisted on four poles, at the head of the school's contingent in the October and May Day parades.

There it was, standing on some boxes. The building, every detail of which they had come to know so well and which meant so much to them, looked almost like the real thing. It was white, with some features in blue and green. There were the two turrets on top of the pilasters. And there were the huge windows of the auditorium and the smaller windows for the rooms— already assigned to somebody or other—on all four floors.

"Maybe we should break it up?" one of the boys asked, avoiding her eyes, and with a guilty expression. "We may as well. There's no room to turn around here as it is."

6

Ivan Grachikov never told wartime stories. He disliked them because during the War he had had more than his share of trouble and very few pleasures. Every day he had lived and every move he had made in the War were linked in his mind with suffering, the sacrifice and the death of decent people.

Another thing he didn't like was that almost twenty years after the end of the War, people were still mouthing the same old military expressions, even where they were quite inappropriate. At the factory he had never used—and he had tried to discourage others from using—such phrases as: "Going over to the offensive," "Throwing people into the breach," "Going over the top," "Bringing up reserves." He felt that all such expressions, which introduced a wartime atmosphere into peacetime conditions, just made people weary. And the Russian language could manage perfectly well without them.

But today he broke his rule about wartime reminiscences. He was sitting with the principal in the reception room of the First Secretary of the Party District Committee and waiting (while in his own reception room, of course, people were also sitting,

77

waiting for *him*). Grachikov was very nervous. He telephoned his secretary a couple of times and smoked two cigarettes. He turned to look at Fyodor, who was sitting there miserable and all hunched up. Grachikov thought that Fyodor's hair was much grayer than it had been the day before. Then, trying to cheer Fyodor up a little, Grachikov started telling him a funny story about some fellows they had both met during a brief lull when their division was resting behind the front line. That was in forty-three, after Fyodor was wounded for the first time.

But the story fell flat. Fyodor did not laugh. Grachikov knew that it was better not to revive war memories. But having started this train of thought, he now recalled what had happened the following day, when his division was suddenly ordered to cross the River Sozh and deploy itself on the other side.

The bridge across the river had been badly damaged. The engineers had repaired it during the night, and Grachikov was posted as the officer in charge of the guard on it. He had instructions that nobody was to be allowed through until the division had crossed over. It was a narrow bridge—the sides had collapsed, the surface was very bumpy, and it was important to keep the traffic moving, because twice already single-engine Junkers had sneaked up on them from behind the trees and dive-bombed the bridge, though so far they had missed. The business of moving the division across, which had begun before dawn, dragged on into the afternoon. Some other units which were also anxious to get across had moved up, but they waited their turn in a small pine woods nearby. Suddenly, six covered vehicles—they were brand-new and all alike—drove up to the head of the column and tried to force their way onto the bridge. "St-o-p!" Grachikov shouted furiously at the first driver and ran across to head him off, but he kept going. Grachikov may have reached for his pistol, perhaps he actually did. At that point a middle-aged officer in a cape opened the door of the first truck and shouted just as furiously. "Hey you, Major. come over here!" and with a quick movement of one shoulder he threw back his cape. And Grachikov saw that he was a Lieutenant-General. Grachikov ran up, his heart in his mouth.

"What were you doing with your hand?" the General shouted ominously. "Do you want to be court-martialed? Let my vehicles through!"

Until the General ordered his trucks to be let through, Grachikov had been willing to settle things amicably, without raising his voice, and he might even have let them through. But when right and wrong clashed head-on (and wrong is more brazen by its very nature), Grachikov's legs seemed to become rooted to the ground and he no longer cared what might happen to him. He drew himself up, saluted, and announced:

"I shall not let you through, Comrade Lieutenant-General!"

"What the hell . . . ?" The General's voice rose to a scream and he stepped down onto the running board. "What's your name?"

"Major Grachikov, Comrade Lieutenant-General. And I'd like to know yours!"

"You'll be in the stockade by tomorrow!" the General fumed.

"That may be, but today you take your place in the line!" Grachikov shot back and then planted himself right in front of the truck and stood there, knowing that his face and neck were flushed purple, but quite determined not to give in. The General choked with rage, thought for a moment, then slammed the door and turned his six trucks around. . . .

At last some people came out of Knorozov's room; they were from the District Agricultural Office and the Agricultural Department of the District Party Committee. Konyevsky, who was Knorozov's secretary (though by his manner and the size of his desk a stranger might well have taken him for Knorozov himself) went into the office and came right out again.

"Victor Vavilovich will see you alone," he said to Grachikov in a tone that brooked no argument.

Grachikov winked at Fyodor and went in.

One of the agricultural people, a livestock expert, was still sitting with Knorozov. His body bent over the desk as though his bones were made of rubber, and his head twisted round as far as it would go, the expert was looking at a large sheet of paper spread out in front of Knorozov. It was covered with brightly colored diagrams and figures.

Grachikov said hello.

Knorozov, a tall man with shaven head, didn't bother to turn toward him, but just threw him a quick glance and said:

"You don't have to worry about agriculture. That's why you can go around wasting other people's time. Why don't you relax?"

He was always needling Grachikov like this about agriculture, as if the town industry, for which Grachikov was responsible, wasn't earning its keep. Grachikov knew that Knorozov was determined to improve the farm situation and get as much credit as possible in the process.

"Look," Knorozov said to the livestock man, slowly pressing the long fingers of one hand on the large sheet of paper, as though he were putting a massive seal on it. He held himself as straight as a die, and didn't lean against the back of the chair. The lines of his body were trim and clean-cut, no matter whether you looked at him from the front or from the side. "Look! I am telling you what you need. What you need is what I'm telling you."

"It's quite clear, Comrade Knorozov," the chief livestock expert said with a bow.

"Take it with you," Knorozov said, letting go of the sheet.

The expert carefully picked up the paper from Knorozov's desk with both hands, rolled it up, and, lowering his head so that his bald patch showed, he strode across the roomy, well-furnished office, which was obviously designed for large conferences.

Thinking that he would be asked to bring in Fyodor almost immediately, Grachikov did not sit down. He just stood leaning against the leather back of the chair in front of him.

Even seated at his desk, Knorozov was a fine figure of a man. His long head made him seem taller, and though he was no longer young, his shaven head, far from aging him, made him look younger. He never seemed to move a muscle without good reason, and he never even changed the expression on his face unless it was necessary. His face seemed cast forever in one mold, never betraying any trivial or momentary emotions. A broad smile would have disarranged his features and destroyed their harmony.

"Victor Vavilovich," Grachikov began, giving

every syllable its full value. His sing-song manner of speech seemed calculated to put people at their ease. "I won't take long. I've come to see you with the principal about the new building for the electronics school. A commission came down from Moscow and said the building is to be handed over to a research institute. Was this done with your knowledge?"

Knorozov did not look at Grachikov. He kept his eyes fixed straight ahead, looking into a far distance that only he could see. He parted his lips—only as much as was necessary—and said brusquely: "Yes."

Actually, this was the end of the conversation.

"Yes?"

"Yes."

It was Knorozov's boast that he never went back on his word. As it had once been in Moscow with Stalin's word, so it was still today with Knorozov's word: It was never changed and never taken back. And although Stalin was long dead, Knorozov was still here. He was a leading proponent of the "strong-willed school of leadership" and he saw in this his greatest virtue. He could not imagine any other way of running things.

Feeling that he was beginning to get worked up, Grachikov forced himself to speak in as friendly and affable a manner as he could.

"But Victor Vavilovich—why don't they build

themselves a place designed for their own needs? In this building they'll have to make no end of alterations."

"No time!" Knorozov cut him short. "The project is already under way. They have to have the place immediately."

"But will it pay its way with all these alterations? And"—he went on quickly, in case Knorozov tried to end the conversation—"and, most important, there's the psychological effect. The students put in a whole year working on that building, without pay and with real enthusiasm . . ."

Knorozov turned his head—just his head, not his shoulders—in Grachikov's direction and, his voice now beginning to sound metallic, he said:

"I don't understand you. You are Secretary of the Town Committee. Do I really have to tell you what's good for the town? We've never had, and we still don't have, a single research institute here. And it wasn't so easy for us to get it. We had to jump at it before the Ministry changed its mind. This puts us into a different class—like Gorki or Sverdlovsk."

He half closed his eyes. Perhaps he was seeing the town transformed into a Sverdlovsk. Or perhaps in his mind's eye he was seeing himself in a new, even more important job.

Grachikov was neither convinced nor crushed by Knorozov's words, which fell like steel girders, and he felt he was coming to one of those critical moments in his life when his legs were rooted to the spot and he had to stand his ground.

Because once again it was a clash of right and wrong.

"Victor Vavilovich," he said more harshly and more curtly than he had intended. "We are not medieval barons, vying with each other over the grandness of our coats of arms. What we should be proud of in this town is that these kids built something and took pleasure in doing it. And it's our job to back them up. But if we take the building from them, they'll never forget what it means to be cheated. They'll think: If it can happen once, it can happen again!"

"There's no point in any further discussion!" The steel girder came down even more heavily than before. "The decision is final!"

A reddish glint came into Grachikov's eyes. His neck and face turned scarlet with anger.

"Look here! What do we care about most—buildings or people?" he shouted. "Why all the fuss about bricks and mortar?"

Knorozov hoisted up the whole great hulk of his body, and you could see that he was truly made of steel and all of a piece.

"Demagogue!" he thundered, towering over the head of the offender.

And he was so powerful a man that it seemed he had

only to stretch out his hand and Grachikov's head would leave his shoulders.

But Grachikov could no longer control himself. He had to keep going.

"Communism has to be built with people, not with bricks, Victor Vavilovich!" he shouted, quite carried away. "That's the hard way, and it takes longer. And even if we finished building Communism tomorrow, but only in bricks, we'd still have a long way to go."

They both fell silent and stood there, stock-still.

Grachikov realized that his fingers hurt. He had dug them into the back of the chair. Now he let go.

"You're not the man for the job," Knorozov said quietly. "We made a mistake."

"All right, I'm not the man for the job. So what?" Grachikov retorted, relieved now that he had spoken his mind. "I can always find work."

"What sort of work?" Knorozov asked suspiciously.

"Any old work! I don't suppose you'll think any the worse of me whatever I do!" Grachikov said at the top of his voice.

He really was sick to death of having to do things without ever being consulted, of always having to take orders from above. He hadn't run things like that back at the factory.

Knorozov made a hissing noise through his clenched teeth.

He put his hand on the telephone.

He lifted the receiver.

Then he sat down.

"Sasha, give me Khabalygin."

While the call was being put through not a word was spoken in the office.

"Khabalygin? Tell me, what are you going to do with this building that needs so many alterations?"

(Sounded as though the building was going to Khabalygin.)

"What do you mean—not very many? There's a lot to be done. . . . I know it's urgent. . . . Anyway, for the time being you've got enough on your hands with one building. . . ."

(Did Khabalygin own the place or something?)

"No, I won't give you the one next to it. You build yourself something better."

He put the receiver down.

"All right, bring the principal in."

Grachikov went out for Fyodor, pondering the thought: Was Khabalygin going to the research institute or something?

He came back in with the principal.

Fyodor stood there rigidly, staring at the District Secretary. He liked him. He had always admired him, and he enjoyed attending meetings called by Knorozov because he felt invigorated by Knorozov's overwhelming will power and energy. Between meetings he put his heart and soul into the execution of Knorozov's wishes—whether it was a matter of improving the work of the school or getting the students to help with the potato harvest or collecting scrap metal or whatever it might be. What Fyodor most liked about Knorozov was that when he said Yes he meant Yes, and when he said No he meant No. The dialectic was all very well, but, like a lot of other people, Fyodor preferred plain and unambiguous language.

So he had not come to argue but simply to learn Knorozov's decision.

"I hear you're having trouble," Knorozov said.

Fyodor smiled wanly.

"Keep your chin up," Knorozov said quietly and firmly. "You're not going to let it get you down, are you?"

"I'm not," Fyodor said hoarsely, and then cleared his throat.

"You've started putting up the dormitory next to the building, haven't you? Once it's up, you'll have a school. Right?"

"Of course, yes," Fyodor agreed.

But this time he didn't feel invigorated by Knorozov's energy. Various thoughts began to go through his mind: Winter was coming, they'd have to stay in the old place for the next year, the new building would have neither an auditorium nor a gymnasium, and there'd be no dormitory adjoining.

"But Comrade Knorozov," Fyodor voiced his worries, "we'll have to alter the whole layout. As they are, the rooms are too small. They're only big enough for four. They'll have to be redesigned for classrooms and labs."

"It's for you to work that out." Knorozov cut him off with an impatient wave of the hand, indicating that the interview was over.

They should have known better than to bother him with such trifling details.

As they walked to the coatrack, Grachikov patted the principal on the shoulder:

"It's not as bad as all that. You'll have a new building."

"We'll have to lay a new floor on top of the basement." The principal kept thinking of all the snags. "It'll have to be much stronger to take the weight of the machinery. That means we'll have to pull down what we've already built of the first story."

"I suppose so," Grachikov said. "But look at it this way. You've got a good plot of land in a good location, already excavated and with foundations. And at least you know where you stand. The place'll be ready by spring and you'll move in. I'll help you, and so will the Economic Council. Lucky thing we managed to hold on to the second building."

They left the District office, both wearing dark raincoats and peaked caps. There was a cool but pleasant breeze and a slight, fresh drizzle.

"By the way," Grachikov asked with a frown, "you wouldn't know by any chance how Khabalygin stands with the Ministry?"

"Khabalygin? O-ho! He's really in with them. He once told me that he's got a lot of friends there. Why, do you think he might put in a word for us?" Fyodor's voice reflected a fleeting hope. But he rejected the idea at once: "No. If he could have helped, he would have done so there and then, when he came around with the commission. But he went along with everything. . . ."

Grachikov stopped, with his feet planted firmly apart, and stared straight ahead. Then he asked another question:

"What's his special field? Relays?"

"Oh, no, he's not an expert on anything. He ran a transformer plant before this. He's just an experienced executive."

"Why did he come along with that commission? Any idea?"

"I wonder." The question now formed in Fyodor's mind, which was still dazed from the events of the previous day. "Why indeed?"

"Well, be seeing you," Grachikov said with a sigh, thrust out his hand, and gave Fyodor a firm handshake.

He went home still thinking about Khabalygin. Of course, this kind of research institute was much grander than a mere relay factory. The director's salary and status would be far greater, and there'd be a good chance of wangling a medal into the bargain.

Grachikov had always been of the opinion that it was wrong to wait until a Party member actually broke the law. He believed that the Party should immediately expel anyone who exploited his job, his position, or his contacts to get something for himself—whether it was a new apartment, a house in the country, or anything at all, however trifling. There was no point in just reproving or reprimanding such people. They had to be expelled, because in their case it was not just a matter of a minor offense or a mistake or personal weakness. Their whole outlook was completely alien: They were really capitalists at heart.

The local newspaper had just exposed and pilloried a truckdriver and his wife who had grown flowers in their back garden and sold them on the market.

But how could you expose the Khabalygins?

Fyodor walked slowly because he wanted to get a breath of fresh air. The lack of sleep, the two Nembutals he had taken, and all the things that had been going through his mind for the last day or so had given him a feeling of discomfort, of being somehow poisoned. But the fresh air gradually blew it away.

Oh well, he thought, we'll just have to start all over again. We'll get all nine hundred of them together and tell them frankly: "We haven't got that building any more. We've got to build another. The harder we work, the sooner we'll have it."

It wasn't going to be easy at first.

But they'd soon be just as enthusiastic as ever about it. That's the effect work always has on people.

They would have faith.

And they would build.

All right, they'd put up with the old place for another year.

And now, before he knew where he was, Fyodor found himself at the new building. It shone with metal and glass.

The other one, next to it, still just a mass of earth and clay, had scarcely gotten above ground level.

Grachikov's questions about Khabalygin had set off a train of half-formed, nagging thoughts in Fyodor's unsuspicious mind, and he was now beginning to piece them together: the way Khabalygin had delayed signing for the building in August, and how cheerful he had been with the commission.

Oddly enough, the first person Fyodor saw on the grounds at the back of the site was the man in his thoughts, the man he had just begun to fathom. Vsevolod Khabalygin, wearing his green hat and a good brown overcoat, was striding about the sodden grounds, ignoring the mud he was getting all over his shoes and giving orders to a group of workmen, apparently his own. Two of the men and a driver were unloading stakes from a truck. Some of the stakes were freshly painted, others were rather grubby, as though they had already been in use—you could tell by their points, which had rotted and then been trimmed again. Two other workmen were bending down and doing something under Khabalygin's direction; he gave his orders with rapid movements of his short arms.

Fyodor went closer and saw that they were driving the stakes into the ground. But they were cheating. Instead of placing them in a straight line, they were being crafty and putting them up in a long, sweeping curve, so as to take in as much of the land as possible for the institute and leave as little as possible for the school.

"Listen, Comrade Khabalygin! Be fair! What's all this?" the principal shouted upon seeing this swindle. "Kids of fifteen and sixteen need space to breathe and run around in! Where will they go?"

At that moment, Khabalygin had planted himself at a strategic spot from which the last section of his misbegotten fence would run. Straddling the future boundary, he had already raised his arm to give the signal when he heard Fyodor just behind him. With his hand still poised at eye level, Khabalygin turned (his thick neck didn't make it easy for him to turn his head), bared his teeth slightly, and snarled:

"What? What do you say?"

And without waiting for an answer, he turned

away, checked the alignment of his men with the palm of his hand, signaled one of them into line by quick movements of his fingers, and finally cut a swathe through the air with a sweep of his short arm.

It was as though he had sliced not just through the air, but the very ground on which he stood. It was the sort of grand gesture that would accompany the opening up of some great new route. It was the gesture of the warrior of ancient times blazing a trail for his armies. It was the gesture of the first mariner to open up a passage to the North Pole.

And only when his task was done did he turn to Fyodor to say:

"That's the way it has to be, dear Comrade."

"Why does it *have* to be?" Fyodor asked angrily, with a shake of his head. "For the good of the cause, I suppose. Is that it? Well, just you wait!" And he clenched his fists. But he could no longer speak. He turned away and strode off quickly toward the road, muttering to himself:

"Just wait, you pig! Just wait, you swine!"

The workmen went on carrying the stakes.

APPENDIX

I. THE OPENING MOVE

WHAT IS "RIGHT"? *

The writing career of the author of *One Day in the Life of Ivan Denisovich* evolved in so dramatic and unusual a manner, and his talent is so individual and so interesting, that nothing which now flows from his pen can fail to excite the liveliest interest. *An Incident at Krechetovka Station* and *Matryona's Home*, whatever your opinion of them, showed that we are in the presence of a gifted writer who has not the slightest intention of confining himself within the limits of the prison-camp theme. Now we have a new story. And, it would appear, a "new" Solzhenitsyn—writing about present-day Party officials, the youth, and so forth. . . .

The words "right" and "wrong" occur several times in Solzhenitsyn's story, and always with special significance and emphasis. "It's all wrong!" shouts one of the story's heroines, while one of the heroes feels that he, too, must proclaim the same thing. And later, in the course of a quarrel that flares up in the office of the Secretary of the District Committee, we read: "Once again it was a clash of right and wrong." This

* *Literaturnaya Gazeta*, No. 105, August 31, 1963.

remark is intended to define the approach to life of one of the characters, but the reader is left in no doubt that it also expresses the author's own point of view on the essence of the conflict.

The conflict revolves around a technical school that is in terrible need of new premises and has those very premises taken away from it and given to a research institute at the last minute, literally on the eve of moving in. Well, is that really just?

Indeed, both teachers and pupils had pinned high hopes on the transfer to the new building: spacious and comfortable lecture halls, well-equipped laboratories and workshops, a dormitory (which meant an end to being scattered all over the place, an end to expensive private accommodations!), a large athletics field, and a big courtyard. . . . So much effort and enthusiasm had been put into the new building by the students, whom the author depicts with much love and sympathy, to speed up the completion of the new building. They themselves had worked on it both before and after classes, on Sundays, and during their vacation. . . . And how we sympathize with the principal, Fyodor Mikheyevich, to whom the loss of the building is a great personal tragedy. His trembling hands are still vividly before my eyes. . . .

Indeed, just a little more and we would cry out together with Lidia, "It's all wrong!" Such is one's first emotional reaction, the first inner response.

Grachikov, the Secretary of the Town Committee, is entirely at the mercy of such emotions. When Fyodor Mikheyevich, his wartime friend, rushes to him in great agitation and asks, in search of support: "Honestly, Ivan, don't you think it's stupid? I don't mean just for the school, but from the point of view of the state, isn't it plain stupid?" Grachikov replies sharply and firmly, without a moment's hesitation: "Yes, it's stupid." And he immediately joins in the battle for the building on the side of the school. It is Grachikov's quarrel with Knorozov, the Secretary of the District Committee, that Solzhenitsyn presents as a clash between right and wrong.

The scene in Knorozov's office is the culminating point of the story. At this juncture, the conflict over the new building becomes more than just a private misunderstanding; it is transplanted from the moral to the political sphere and is interpreted by Solzhenitsyn as a conflict between two styles of Party work, between two political lines: Lenin's and the one that was decisively condemned at the Twentieth Congress.

Who is this Knorozov?—"As it had once been in Moscow with Stalin's word, so it was still today with Knorozov's word: It was never changed and never taken back. And, although Stalin was long dead, Knorozov was still here. He was a leading proponent of the 'strong-willed school of leadership' and he saw in this his greatest virtue. He could not imagine any other way of running things." Solzhenitsyn depicts Knorozov with sharp, almost caricature touches ("His face seemed cast forever in one mold, never betraying any trivial or momentary emotions. . . . He was truly made of steel and all of a piece." His voice is "metallic," his words fall "like steel girders.") not bothering to portray him as a real, living person; we see him not so much as a human being, but as a symbol of the era of the cult of personality.

There is far more of the real and the individual in Grachikov, but he and Knorozov are contrasted by the author not just as individuals but as new types: the new Party official as opposed to an embodiment of the methods of leadership typical of the period of the cult of personality. Solzhenitsyn several times refers to such qualities of Grachikov's as his democratic way of working, consideration for people, his ability to hear them out and to work, as Grachikov says, "in the Soviet way." . . . "Grachikov much preferred to decide things without rushing—giving himself time to think and letting others have a say." Such qualities are indeed excellent, and the author's attempt to understand the new type of Party leader as a product of our times is worthy of every encouragement. But the trouble is that Grachikov's actions and behavior are completely at variance with this intention.

What is the distinguishing feature of the Party official

of today? It is primarily the effort to analyze profoundly and to understand the *essence* of any problem, to get down to its roots and to grasp its meaning in all its complex relationship with the world around it. But there is not the slightest suggestion of anything like this in Grachikov. We are presented with an impulsive person who surrenders easily to fleeting emotions and makes rash, irresponsible decisions. It is strange that, having learned of the proposed transfer of the building to the institute, Grachikov does not even try to probe the merits of the affair and ponder it seriously. After all, the Secretary of the Town Committee knows perfectly well that the institute is "important." ("Once you know that its address is a P.O. box number, you don't ask any questions.") . . . Incidentally, the following detail is typical: While the author rightly condemns Yakov Ananyevich, the Secretary of the school's Party Buro (by the way, this episodic figure in the story is sketched laconically but extremely effectively), who is not prepared to speak frankly to the students and explain to them what has happened, he does not seem to mind that it does not occur to Grachikov (or, incidentally, to Fyodor Mikheyevich) to take this logical and very important step, which could well have taken the edge off the sharpness of the conflict. Furthermore, something that can be excused in the principal, who is blinded by his sense of grievance and who is thrown off balance, is quite inexcusable in the Secretary of the Town Committee. What sort of "Soviet" work is that?

No, if we are going to talk about a new type of leader, then Grachikov as depicted in the story is the last person to be pitted against a Knorozov. The day of such people as Knorozov is past—and there Solzhenitsyn is absolutely right—but he has not succeeded in describing those who are actually taking their place.

In Solzhenitsyn's story there is one circumstance that, in his opinion, provides ample justification for resolving the question of "right" and "wrong" as Grachikov and Fyodor Mikheyevich see it. This is the personal involvement of Knorozov and Khabalygin, the director of the relay factory, in the transfer of the building to the research institute. The former dreams of the elevation of "his" town to a higher status and of the consequent enhancement of his own power; the latter counts on being put in charge of the new institute.

It is interesting to note, however, that both Grachikov and Fyodor Mikheyevich express their opinion of the proposed transfer of the building to the institute even *before* they learn of Khabalygin's careerist ambitions. Moreover, the very appointment of the non-specialist Khabalygin ("He ran a transformer plant before this. He's just an experienced executive.")

to the directorship of a major scientific research institute does not look very credible, it must be said.

But even this is not the most important aspect. Most
important of all is that neither Knorozov's ambitions
nor Khabalygin's careerism can obscure, nor ought
they to obscure, the basic questions, which must be
answered if talk of "right" and "wrong" is ever to
emerge from the sphere of general abstraction. After
all, is it right, is it possible, is it reasonable to discuss
seriously whether the outcome is right or wrong without having a clear idea of what exactly the new institute is, what significance it has, whether its immediate
opening is dictated by pressing necessity, whether it
isn't just possible that the school's interests will be
safeguarded, and so forth?

Unfortunately, not only those characters in the
story whom the author presents as positive heroes, but
the author himself for some reason, avoid these
questions. The phrase "for the good of the cause,"
which Solzhenitsyn has made the title of his story, has
an obviously sarcastic undertone—the words are discredited by the demagogue Khabalygin. Yet these
words are not only mouthed by demagogues; they
have a real, and most important, meaning. But this is
completely ignored by the author. So what happens?
Real, living bonds and relationships are destroyed, and
we are presented with an artificially constructed,

imaginary world, where honest, decent, but weak-willed champions of justice are found to be helpless, not so much in the face of the Knorozovs and Khabalygins as in the face of some indifferent, unfeeling force, which can be sensed behind the faceless, nameless representatives of unnamed institutions ("a Comrade from the Department of . . ." and "the Head of the Electronics Section from . . .").

It would be wrong to suppose that these serious defects in the very conception of Solzhenitsyn's story do not affect its literary qualities. Truth to life is an intellectual and aesthetic category, and the slightest deviation from it is fraught with failure in the "purely" artistic sphere. Here and there in the story *For the Good of the Cause*, in the occasional vivid touches or observations or in a particular word, we can detect the hand of Solzhenitsyn, but the plasticity and organic qualities of the language which won us over in the best pages of his other prose are lacking on this occasion.

And so, it's a failure. . . . But is there a single artist, and especially an artist who is still trying to find his way, who is immune to failure?

Of course not.

And maybe it would not be worth talking about this failure of Solzhenitsyn's if the shortcomings of this story did not have much in common with what the critics noted in, for example, *Matryona's Home*. I refer to his attempts to resolve the most complex intellectual and moral problems, to pass judgments on people and their actions, without reference to actual, living relationships; he operates in abstract categories which are not invested with a concrete social content. In *Matryona's Home* it was the "righteous woman" without whom neither the village nor the town nor "our whole land" was supposed to be worth anything. In this story it is the "little" people who have racked their brains in fruitless efforts to answer a scholastic question, posed without reference to space or time: What *is* "right"?

It might seem that *For the Good of the Cause* is the most topical of Solzhenitsyn's stories. But if you think it over and ignore such completely extraneous features as the sailboats and palmtrees on the shirts, the short crew cuts, and the "supermodern" views of the young people on literature—if all this is thrown out— then the writer's views of life and his attitude toward it will be seen to have remained just as un-modern, and in many respects as archaic, as they were in *Matryona's Home*. We have not found the "new," truly modern Solzhenitsyn here.

And yet we are undoubtedly in the presence of a writer of great and honest quality who is uniquely sensitive to any manifestation of evil or untruth or injustice. This is a great force, but only when it is combined with a knowledge and deep understanding of the laws governing the movement of the real world and an ability to see clearly the direction of that movement.

I think and I believe that our encounter with the "new" Solzhenitsyn is still to come.

YURI BARABASH

II. COUNTERMOVE

IS THE CRITIC RIGHT? *

It so happened that I read Yuri Barabash's review of Solzhenitsyn's *For the Good of the Cause* before reading the story itself. As a result, I approached the story with an unconscious prejudice, having been put on my guard by the serious criticism contained in what seemed a convincing review—all the more so since it was written in a tone of quiet good will that inspired confidence. However, Solzhenitsyn made me change my mind, convinced me of the rightness of his case, and, moreover, made me take up my pen and enter into a polemical debate, despite my lack of experience as a critic.

As far as I understand Barabash, his main objection to the story is this: that the author, and, consequently, the reader, cannot pass judgment on the justice or injustice of the handing over of the school's new premises to the scientific research institute without knowing

* *Literaturnaya Gazeta*, No. 124, October 15, 1963.

how urgent is the need for this institute, whether it would be possible to do it without violating the interests of the school, and so forth—that is, without knowing the actual circumstances in the light of which such questions have to be decided. . . .

The demand that we should be kept informed of the real circumstances is a perfectly legitimate one. Indeed, just put yourself in the place of Fyodor Mikheyevich, the principal of the school and the person most deeply interested in the new premises; in Fyodor Mikheyevich's place every one of us would probably approve of the impending action if its necessity were explained to us honestly and straightforwardly—that is, if I, as principal of the school, had been informed of the circumstances that would permit me to judge whether such a decision was "for the good of the cause" or not. And here I have in mind the national cause, the cause for which one can readily sacrifice one's own interest.

It is possible theoretically to imagine a matter of such importance to the state: a research institute has to be situated in a specific town, and moreover at once, and no other premises are available, nobody else can be moved out, and so forth. After weighing all these circumstances, even Fyodor Mikheyevich, even Lidia Georgievna, yes, even the young people themselves— that is, people who are aware of other considerations, unknown in all their complexity "at the highest level" —would have resolved the problem correctly and given up their building to the research institute.

But therein lies the trouble: No one explains *all* the circumstances to Fyodor Mikheyevich and no one draws him into the whole affair. Nobody bothers about him: they just tell him that's how it has to be— "For the good of the cause."

If we think of it not as a theoretical but as a real situation, then I admit that it is rather difficult to imagine that today such an emergency could arise—the need to accommodate a *new* (!) research institute in a school building not designed for it, and where the premises have to be altered at about half the cost of the whole building. We know that the setting up of a new research institute is not usually decided so simply or so quickly. The fuss being made about the new building and Khabalygin's behavior put us on our guard from the very beginning.

However, anything is possible, and the critic is justified in demanding evidence, for the commission's decision might indeed serve the good of the cause! But let us look and see whether the author really does not give us a chance of drawing our own conclusions on the justice or injustice of the whole business.

In actual fact, Grachikov, the Secretary of the Town Committee, had long known that they were planning to open a research institute. There had been talk about it early in the spring, but the decision had been delayed.

It was held up, and therefore Grachikov quite properly drew the conclusion that there was no need for such haste and that it was prompted by anything but considerations of state. In any case, Grachikov knows more about this research institute than we do or the principal, and when, in reply to the principal's question, "Honestly, Ivan, don't you think it's stupid? I don't mean just for the school, but from the point of view of the state, isn't it plain stupid?" Grachikov replies: "Yes, it's stupid," I certainly don't see before me, to quote Barabash, "an impulsive person, surrendering easily to fleeting emotions, and making rash, irresponsible decisions."

On the contrary, I see Grachikoy quite differently: calm and immovable when he knows what *has* to be done and what should *not* be done. That is what he was like during the War when he stopped the General's car at the bridge, and that is what he is like now in Knorozov's office. Yes, he does indeed set off to see Knorozov immediately and without hesitation (as Barabash notes with some disapproval), but he does so because he believes the transfer of the school building to be wrong.

What is the main argument that Knorozov offers him? "We've never had, and we still don't have, a single research institute here. And it wasn't so easy for us to get it. We had to jump at it before the Ministry changed its mind. This puts us into a different class—like Gorki or Sverdlovsk."

So this, it turns out, is the crux of the matter! It's not a question of urgency or planning, but of the most parochial, selfish interests imaginable. This means that there was no imperative necessity for putting the research institute into that town. This means it could have been set up in another town without any material or moral harm to the state. This means that the Ministry could still change its mind, and that it was urgent only for Knorozov, and not in the interests of science. It is quite likely that the research institute (although this is really irrelevant to this situation) is also under cruel pressure, that it must be opened as soon as possible, and the need for it may be extremely great, yet Knorozov got the institute, and with great difficulty, for himself, into "his" town. . . .

These are the circumstances and the motivations that entitle us to weigh and pass judgment on the rightness of Grachikov's and Fyodor Mikheyevich's attitude and the good of their cause—which turns out to be the great, true cause—as well as on the "rightness" of the petty, selfish cause of Knorozov.

Grachikov and Fyodor Mikheyevich go to see Knorozov, hoping for a reasonable solution of the conflict. One cannot demand that they should explain to the students what has happened *before* having had this conversation. *After* their talk with Knorozov, how could they explain it, when neither of them agreed with his decision and thought it wrong?

Incidentally, I must admit that in the passage where Grachikov and Fyodor Mikheyevich are returning from their interview with Knorozov, I find Grachikov's comforting words somewhat jarring, and on this point I cannot refrain from agreeing with Barabash: The weakness and helplessness of the champion of justice are upsetting. But I ask myself: Do I have the right to address this reproach to the author? Maybe it is Grachikov himself who evokes this irritation. Where is it said that we are faced with a model of the new type of leader? And why must we go along with Barabash and believe that Solzhenitsyn is here contrasting Grachikov with Knorozov saying: Here is a leader of the *new* type, and here is the *old* type of leader. Such contrasts are possible only in that artificially constructed, unreal world which Barabash criticizes.

All the same it is difficult for me to be entirely on Solzhenitsyn's side in this. Grachikov's consoling remarks contain an element of untruth. He wants to inspire Fyodor Mikheyevich with some hope—but hope of what? Of a compromise?

Is it that Grachikov considers any further struggle useless? Where does this submissiveness come from, and why does he abandon his principles, after such determined, even desperate, actions? At this point in the story I simply do not have sufficient material to understand what is taking place in this man's mind or to follow the emotional aspect of his behavior. I fear that there is some sort of gap here, and as a reader, I found myself unable to bridge it. It is true that Grachikov tries to fathom Khabalygin. He is convinced that Khabalygin must be driven out of the Party, and it is evident that he will continue to fight him. But even in this one senses a sort of evasion, a sort of failure to develop Grachikov's character completely.

The story cannot be discussed without considering the moral issue involved. The students have been cheated. They have not only had their building taken away; their enthusiasm, their faith, and their dreams have been shattered. This is what Lidia Georgievna reacts to so sharply and so painfully and what Grachikov gives little thought to, since he is to a certain extent satisfied at least to have managed to hold on to part of the site.

But this compromise is purely administrative and cannot resolve the moral conflict. In any case, what *could* compensate for the moral loss inflicted on the young minds? Working only "for the good of the cause" and not for the good of people as well is contrary to the principles of Communist ethics. In Knorozov's ossified mind these two concepts are completely and utterly dissociated. For him the concept of the "cause" does not include the interests of the individual, the interests of the people—and by that is meant not just people in general, but real people with real desires and sorrows.

So the question of right and wrong is certainly not posed abstractly in the story, outside time and space. The democratization of our life has been marked in recent years by efforts to do everything possible to widen participation in the administration, in supervisory work, and likewise in Party and Soviet work. There are people who are upset by this democratization. Why? How do they act, what are their tactics, their methods, what is their philosophy? This is the object of Solzhenitsyn's interest.

Seriously and courageously he poses a moral and social problem: What does "for the good of the cause" mean? He raises this problem to the level of the high moral demands of a Communist society. He fights passionately for faith in the people who are furthering that cause and who alone have the right to judge what is useful to the cause and what is not. He exposes those who, while using the interests of the state as a cover, look after their own little affairs at the expense of the state. He demands justice, and how can one call his approach "scholastic" when he is trying to defend justice and further it? Only a story filled with the joy and the pain that come from real knowledge of life can excite and move us in this way.

It would be ridiculous for me to claim that all my

judgments are unassailable. Like any other work of art, this story examines life in all its complexity and contradictions. And various interpretations and objections may arise. But they must at least deal with what is actually in the story.

DMITRI GRANIN

III. THE ATTACK DEVELOPS

BEHIND THE TIMES *

. . . Yes, all sorts of things happen in real life. I myself know of a school that was "moved out" of premises belonging to it. But in that case it was quite obvious that the motives for the decision really were unjust. It happened near Leningrad and it became known immediately—as it was bound to, for today that sort of thing gets out right away. Such actions invariably run into firm opposition on the part of the general public. All the forces of our democratic system at once come into play, and people start banging on every door in their efforts to see justice done. Can that atmosphere of passivity and helplessness described by Solzhenitsyn exist today in any community? I don't think so. At least not in any of the educational communities with whose life I am acquainted. That is why it is difficult to sense in Solzhenitsyn's story any

* *Literaturnaya Gazeta,* October 19, 1963.

feeling for the life of today. It seems rather to evoke echoes of life the day before yesterday. . . . It is not inertia or passivity that is characteristic of Soviet man; nor are these features typical of our public life. Genuine justice, fought for and won by the Party and our whole people—and not "abstract" justice—runs through our life today and is triumphant!

A writer who takes it upon himself to deal with an important contemporary theme cannot fail to take all this into account.

R. N. SELIVERSTOV

THE EDITORS SPEAK

(Seliverstov's article was accompanied by a statement from the editors of *Literaturnaya Gazeta*.)

In publishing Yuri Barabash's article "What Is 'Right'?" the editors felt—and still feel—that the critic's comments on Solzhenitsyn's story were well founded. In his article "Is the Critic Right?" Dmitri Granin voices another point of view about the story. This paper printed Granin's article in the belief that the exchange of differing opinions on problems of literature is useful in itself. Today, having previously published a critic and a writer, we have given space to a reader. It seems to the editors that R. N. Seliverstov makes valid comments on Solzhenitsyn's story and Granin's article.

Solzhenitsyn's story obviously would not in itself have provided material for a continuing discussion had not some general questions of principle—primarily the question of the class approach versus the "universal," extrasocial approach to the concepts of humanism and justice—arisen in the course of the debate. These problems have attracted the attention of the critics and of our readers.

In letters received by the editors there is support for the author's criticism of people like Knorozov and Khabalygin. It is impossible not to agree with the opinion of one of the readers, the engineer Y. Dunaevsky of Baltisk, who, while paying tribute to Solzhenitsyn's talent, writes: "While duly appreciating the author's talents, one should not simultaneously extol his mistakes. . . . I believe that he will find in himself sufficient strength to imbue people not with hopelessness, but with confidence in the strength of justice, confidence that, although there are still quite a few Khabalygins and Knorozovs about, they are no longer all-powerful, and that the battle against them is a legitimate one. . . ."

It is exactly this that many of his readers would like to see in Solzhenitsyn's future works. We must hope that their criticism and advice will help the writer.

A keen ideological battle is going on in the modern world. And we must not for a single moment lower our ideological and ethical standards in our assessment of literary works. It is because we respect a writer's talent that we cannot make allowances for his artistic mistakes.

Soviet art knows no limitations in the choice of subject matter. All aspects of life are open to it, including the negative ones. But a socialist-realist artist handles themes from the standpoint of the Communist view of the world.

THE EDITORS

IV. THE COUNTERATTACK: OLD BOLSHE-VIKS, THE DIALECTIC, WORKERS *

AN AUTHOR'S SUCCESS

We, former Party propagandists, have always believed that it is very important to support everything that is truthful and just, as the Party teaches us.

And this is particularly important at the present time, when our whole people is building Communism —the most just society on earth.

Alexander Solzhenitsyn is absolutely right when he stresses this side of the question in his story *For the Good of the Cause,* where it is a matter of such vital importance for this large and fine group of nine hundred young men and women standing on the threshold of life. This is not an abstract presentation of the question, as Yuri Barabash mistakenly supposes,

* *Novy Mir,* No. 10, October, 1963.

but a very important problem of bringing up young people in the spirit of the Party's teachings. Such things ought not to be forgotten, especially by a literary critic.

Barabash's ironic remarks on the title of the story, *For the Good of the Cause*, are irrelevant. The author of the story is right. In reality, petty bureaucrats (and there are still plenty of them, and quite unreformed ones, in our country) frequently conceal their bureaucratic desires and actions by imaginary "considerations of state" and by appeals to "the good of the cause." Here Solzhenitsyn exposes just such a situation.

The transfer of the building, put up for the school, to the research institute meant not only the brutal disregard of the rights of the young people to the new premises (and their claims were just, because the building had been built to a large extent by these same young people), but also involved the additional expenditure by the state of a million and a half rubles for alterations. And all this supposedly "for the good of the cause," though actually because of the ambitions of one man and the careerism of another.

It is truly impossible to understand why Barabash found it necessary to take upon himself the defense of this kind of "national interest."

As for the two different styles of Party leadership, we are against Knorozov's "iron-fisted" style, which smacks strongly of the style known in the period of the

Stalin cult. We are in favor of Grachikov's style and we are not afraid of his "excessive" goodness, his genuinely Leninist affection for people and his concern for them, because this is what is most important in Party work. Goodness does not exclude the upholding of high principles or purposeful efficiency in leadership. The unforgettable example and the whole life's work of Vladimir Ilyich Lenin is sufficient affirmation of this.

We, old Communists, consider that articles such as that of Barbash lead large numbers of readers astray —especially our young people.

So it turns out in fact that Solzhenitsyn's supposed "failure," which Barabash writes about, is nothing of the sort. On the contrary, *For the Good of the Cause* is another success both for the author and for us, the readers.

Y. YAMPOLSKAYA, member of the CPSU since 1917
I. OKUNYEVA, member of the CPSU since 1919
M. GOLDBERG, member of the CPSU since 1920

AN OPEN LETTER TO YURI BARABASH

Dear Comrade Barabash,

You were the first to comment in *Literaturnaya Gazeta* on Solzhenitsyn's story *For the Good of the Cause*, and on the whole you are right in demanding that an artist should deal with highly controversial moral problems in a concrete, historical manner and should not allow them to be diluted, so to speak, in high-minded abstractions. This demand would evoke sympathy and support if certain of your arguments did not themselves suffer from abstractness and if they were not extremely controversial.

"What Is 'Right'?"—This is the title of your article, but you fail to answer the question. Do you really in all seriousness believe that it is entirely just to hand over the classrooms built collectively by students and teachers of a school to a research institute on the sole grounds that the institute must be of vital importance? (After all, this institute had not yet been opened; it was still in the process of looking for premises.)

The question is not, of course, a simple one, though in the old days such a question would not have been a problem at all. When one man exercised his despotic will, then the interests of the country and the interests of the many were often ignored. But times have changed. Let us then examine the question, thinking primarily of the story as told by the author himself.

You, Comrade Barabash, charge Solzhenitsyn with being abstract. And even when you quote him, you fail to observe how concrete his thought is. Just judge for yourself: Is Solzhenitsyn really so abstract? Here is Fyodor Mikheyevich speaking to Grachikov:

"Honestly, Ivan, don't you think it's stupid? I don't mean just for the school, but *from the point of view of the state*, isn't it plain stupid?"

It is precisely from the point of view *of the state* (and not abstractly) that Solzhenitsyn tries to resolve these controversial moral issues. But it looks as if you, Comrade Barabash, are not trying to see this. It emerges extremely clearly from the story what the point of view *of the state* amounts to: The building was designed for the school—well-lit and spacious classrooms had been built for the nine hundred students (who had been working in cramped, unsuitable quarters); the new premises had been specially equipped for the laboratories and studies; there were special workshops with concrete floors for the heavy machinery, a gymnasium, a cloakroom for the students, and so forth. The story speaks about all this precisely and in great detail. To alter this building to meet the needs of the research institute, great sums would have to be spent, and these funds would be spent on destroying what had been done—that is, in an anti-state manner. The point of view of the *state* in Solzhenitsyn is primarily a concrete, economic point of view; it is the battle against that inefficiency which distinguished certain other "administrators" who flourished in the atmosphere of the personality cult.

But in taking the point of view of the state, the writer is not limited to this. His view is both deep and broad, and he links economic questions to questions of ideology and morals. He shows us that anti-state activity in the economy (in this particular instance it was a matter of capital outlay) is motivated by careerism, lack of principles, and disregard for people, for their work and their studies, their present and their future.

Now you, Comrade Barabash, say you are surprised that neither the principal of the school nor the Secretary of the Town Committee showed any pressing desire to talk to the students, to speak frankly to them, though such a conversation, in your opinion, would have been able to take the edge off the sharpness of the conflict. But really, you are proposing a very strange, controversial (not to say unpedagogic) solution. Solzhenitsyn does not have to take the edge off the conflict, because for his characters there can be no reconciliation between right and wrong. Lidia says that to deprive the students of the new building would be to cheat them. And such honest people as Lidia, Fyodor Mikheyevich, and **Grachikov** are *quite unable* to play any part in this deception. In this instance to "explain" to the students the "necessity" of handing over their building to the institute would be possible only by resorting to demagogy and lies. And, if this whole deal is against the interests of the state, then such lies would only be an ideological aiding and abetting of that anti-state act. And what would be the effect on the students, now cheated a second time? Their young minds would be outraged by the injustice, and it would be all the more cruel because this injustice and this anti-state act had been committed by people on whom they depend and whom they have to obey.

The reality, concreteness, and profundity of the moral issue in the story are rooted in the direct connection established between inefficient administration and demagogy and lies, which may have (and in fact do have) the most damaging effect on young minds.

Comrade Barabash, you declare one-sidedly and unjustly: "The phrase 'for the good of the cause,' which Solzhenitsyn has made the title of his story, has an obviously sarcastic undertone—the words are discredited by the demagogue Khabalygin. Yet these words are not only mouthed by demagogues; they have a real, and most important, meaning. But this is *completely ignored by the author*." Those words of yours which I have italicized are particularly strange and paradoxical. After all, the story was written in order to reveal the difference between demagogy, pragmatism, and careerism on the one hand, and, on the other, that world of ideas and feelings which exists and must develop and must triumph *for the good of the cause*, of the country, and of people. The *whole* story serves this purpose. It was written for your good and for mine, and for all of us. The most important issues are not "completely ignored" by the writer; they are reaffirmed by the imagery and the conflicts and borne out by the high-mindedness of the fight (by no means an easy one) for the highest interests of the state, for the victory of the common cause.

You did not see in the story any "real, living bonds," though you saw an "imaginary world, where honest, decent, but weak-willed champions of justice are found to be helpless . . . in the face of some indifferent, unfeeling force. . . ." But why, in your frame of reference, are these "honest, decent champions of justice" relegated to an imaginary world, and why are the very tangible scoundrels, ruthless crooks, and degenerate bureaucrats characterized vaguely as "some unfeeling force"? Is it really possible to misrepresent so arbitrarily the thoroughly concrete images and thoughts of the writer? And why do you include Grachikov, Lidia, and Fyodor Mikheyevich among the "little people" who allegedly "racked their brains in fruitless efforts to answer the question . . . What *is* 'right'?" Once again you are inaccurate, you again misinterpret arbitrarily the real meaning of the characters and situations. Solzhenitsyn's story is not a medieval tract about good and evil, but a very concrete work, the essence of which has already been discussed. Fyodor Mikheyevich is by no means preoccupied with solving the "question" of right and wrong (remember, he does not even utter these words). He is completely a man of this world, unselfishly absorbed in his own cause, and he is far less concerned with talking than with doing and *fighting*. How could you classify him and Grachikov as "little people"?

For goodness' sake, have you forgotten the end of the story? Fyodor Mikheyevich there threatens Khabalygin ("Just wait, you swine," he says to him), and it is quite clear that the "little" principal is by no means "little," but a real, life-sized man, that he is not broken (times have changed) but, on the contrary, inspired by righteous anger, he is fighting and will go on fighting until he wins.

You included Grachikov among the "little people," though at the same time you say quite rightly that the scene in the office of the Secretary of the District Committee is treated by Solzhenitsyn as a conflict between two styles of Party work and two political lines: the Leninist one and the one that was decisively condemned at the Twentieth Congress.

How can Grachikov, who stands for the Leninist style of Party work, be described as a "little person"? In essence you put yourself on the side of Knorozov: After all, it was he, Knorozov, who decided, brutally and irrevocably, what must be done "for the good of the cause."

Knorozov had already decided on (and had already issued instructions about) the transfer of the new building to the still nonexistent research institute, and you, Comrade Barabash, have agreed with this. I cannot see your logic. If the personality cult and everything connected with it are to be condemned, then we must get right to the root of it and clearly expose the improper methods to which the Knorozovs resort, thereby discrediting and damaging our great cause.

Incidentally, in drawing attention to Knorozov's careerism and despotism, you claim that the writer has been little concerned about "portraying him as a real, living person." But don't you see that the Knorozovs have *no* living features (on the ideo-aesthetic level)? They are petrified bureaucrats. On the other hand, the truly living Grachikov was not to your liking. You did not see in him a "real Party official." This makes odd reading. . . . The sincerity, the warmth, and the ability to become fearlessly "rooted to the ground" (without concern for his own safety and well-being), to risk his life for a just cause, and to join a bitter battle —and what a difficult one!—with people like Knorozov: Did you not notice any of this? You make practically no reference to the text of the story when you criticize Grachikov. I will also not quote—my letter is long enough as is—but I believe that if you read Solzhenitsyn's story once again (and the work of a great and complex writer has to be read more than once, even by a very experienced reader), you will see that a truly typical Communist of the Leninist type, a man of high principles, shines through Grachikov's remarkable, unique personality.

You are right when you call Solzhenitsyn a writer of

great and honest quality. And there can be no argument that every talented writer should be subjected to serious criticism. But you will agree that a great talent deserves above all a positive interpretation.

A major talent is almost always complex, demanding of the critic great care, I would even say delicacy. And least of all, it seems to me, should one judge the work of such a talented author with the sort of finality that brooks no argument, as you have done in labeling *For the Good of the Cause* a "failure."

For the Good of the Cause is typical of Solzhenitsyn—taut, tragic, and at the same time optimistic. Solzhenitsyn's story is evidence of the increased vigor of our literature, of its profound impact on life and on the most controversial developments in the world at large, and of the growth of our sense of social responsibility. And in these conditions it is becoming ever more difficult for all sorts of degenerates and careerists, dogmatists and demagogues to survive, because people like Grachikov, Lidia, and Fyodor Mikheyevich are becoming steadily stronger. I am sure that *for the good of the cause* and for the sake of justice (that is, for the sake of the national interest), we must offer every kind of support to a talented writer when he appears in our midst and explain the strength of his talent and his works, and not lead readers astray through categorical and basically inaccurate and unjust criticism. That is why I have written this letter and I hope that you will understand me and agree with me.

L. REZNIKOV
Lecturer at the University of Petrozavodsk

"IS THAT THE WAY?"

It occurs to us that in assessing the specific situation described by Solzhenitsyn, Barabash is a victim of the demogogy of people like Khabalygin, who are past masters at pursuing their own selfish aims under the guise of defending the national interest.

In our view it is men like Grachikov and the principal, Fyodor Mikheyevich, who defend the interests of the nation, not the Khabalygins with their predatory methods. Unfortunately, one still hears of cases of people like Knorozov and Khabalygin . . . supposedly "for the good of the cause" cutting down forests, polluting reservoirs, or ruining expensive instruments by the removal of some small part which they need. In other words, they skim the cream off the milk.

The attempt by Khabalygin and his influential protectors to take the building away from the school is quite on a par with this sort of behavior. In the decisions of the Twenty-second Congress of the CPSU and in the speeches of N. S. Khrushchev, there is one thought that occurs over and over again: We have finished with the days when no price was too great for

economic development. The Party is waging a relentless battle against the irrational and uneconomic expenditure of national funds and is focusing attention
on the economics of production and construction.

It is difficult, therefore, to understand how one can
talk seriously of the good of a "cause" that requires
alterations on a scarcely finished building to the tune
of nearly one and a half times the cost of the original
construction. . . .

We thus have a clash between the bureaucratic
methods of yesterday, the approach which was so
familiar in the period of the personality cult, and the
democratic foundations of Soviet life today. That is
why Barabash is absolutely wrong when he states that
the justice for which Solzhenitsyn's heroes fight is
abstract and outside time and place. . . .

Some people may object that the question of where
and how soon the new institute is to be set up is outside
the competence of the teachers, and certainly of the
students, of the school whose building is being taken
away. Of course, this is something that cannot be
decided by a general vote. But in the given circumstances—the new building has been put up with the
participation of the people involved, and an enthusiastic community has formed around this common cause
—it was absolutely imperative, both on ethical and on
political grounds, that the question be decided in con-
sultation with this collective, and not behind its back.

Let us suppose for a moment, however, that there are compelling arguments in favor of depriving the school of its new building and of forcing it to continue working for another year or two in abnormal conditions. We have no doubt that any Soviet or Komsomol collective would understand and would arrive at a correct decision. But nobody must be permitted to defile the pure enthusiasm of those fine young boys and girls, with their shining faith in justice and their legitimate pride in their work.

That is not the way. That is wrong, says Solzhenitsyn in a story that defends our Soviet, Communist justice, the ethical norms of the moral code, and the democratic foundations of our life.

V. SHEINIS
Lathe operator in the Kirov factory,
shock-worker of Communist labor

R. TSIMERINOV
T-crane operator

V. END GAME AND CHECKMATE: REPLIES AND FINAL REBUTTAL *

The editors of *Novy Mir* have had their say in this controversy [about Solzhenitsyn's work] by publishing three letters from readers.

* *Literaturnaya Gazeta*, No. 148, December 12, 1963, and No. 154, December 26, 1963.

There appears to us to be no particular need to iterate what has already been said by the editors of *Literaturnaya Gazeta* about the commendable vigor of the story's attack on bureaucracy and officialdom, as well as the work's serious failings: They were dealt with in detail in Barabash's article and Seliverstov's letter.

We would simply like to point out that the editors of *Literaturnaya Gazeta* provided an opportunity for *different* opinions about Solzhenitsyn's story to be voiced in its pages, feeling it only natural that at the end they should express their editorial opinion as well. The editors of *Novy Mir* apparently consider this type of discussion too democratic. The letters *they* have published contain only unqualified praise of the story and are unanimous in their attacks on the author of the critical article in *Literaturnaya Gazeta*.

It stands to reason that the opportunities which a magazine has for praising works which it publishes are truly unlimited. But it is scarcely necessary to point out that this is done at great cost—at the expense of objectivity and a sense of proportion.

We have no reason whatsoever to doubt the sincerity of the authors of the contributions published in *Novy Mir*. What is strange, however, is that, in making their selection of letters, the editors found it impossible to mention, let alone to publish, any readers' letters containing criticisms of the story. It is difficult to believe (and this is borne out by *Literaturnaya Gazeta*'s own mail) that the editors of *Novy Mir* received only letters singing the story's praises. . . .

In this connection we would like to say the following: Any editorial board is responsible not only to its readers; it also bears a moral responsibility toward the writer whose work it publishes. It is the sacred duty of editors to help a writer, to draw attention to his weak points, and help him to overcome them. In summing up the discussion about *Novy Mir*'s statement on Solzhenitsyn's story, it is worth pointing out that true respect for a writer excludes any form of indulgence toward his weaknesses and errors as an artist. . . .

(The December 26, 1963, issue of *Literaturnaya Gazeta* printed a reply by the editors of *Novy Mir*. After summarizing the debate and quoting the essential passages from *Literaturnaya Gazeta*'s comments, *Novy Mir*'s letter continued:)

Thus the editors of the magazine [*Novy Mir*] are in effect being accused of misrepresenting the views of its readers. This compels us to give an account of the mail which the magazine has received about Solzhenitsyn's story.

The editors of *Novy Mir* received a total of fifty-eight letters dealing with *For the Good of the Cause*. Many of them amount in effect to long articles of between ten and twenty typed pages of detailed argument. The authors of fifty-five letters, three of which we published, thoroughly approve of Solzhenitsyn's story and take issue with his critics. . . .

It should be pointed out that twelve of these letters were carbon copies of originals sent to *Literaturnaya Gazeta*. This is the case with two of the letters which we printed. In view of this, *Literaturnaya Gazeta*'s chosen method of conducting a debate is hardly likely to strike anybody as "too democratic." Of course, any editorial board is free to disagree with the majority of its readers about the value of a work and may express a contrary opinion. But in that case, this probably ought to be done openly and the readers should have the mistakenness of their views explained to them, rather than have their views misrepresented in this manner.

And now for that part of *Novy Mir*'s mail containing "critical comments" on Solzhenitsyn's story, which *Literaturnaya Gazeta* demanded that we publish. Two letters contain comments on the language used in the story. . . .

Only one of the fifty-eight letters (from N. L. Marchenko, railroad station Udelnaya, Moscow region) expresses disapproval of Solzhenitsyn's story. However, there is not a word in this letter about the actual content of the story, its subject or its characters. It was apparently only an excuse for the writer to condemn Solzhenitsyn's work as a whole. N. L. Marchenko considers the publication of any of Solzhenitsyn's works as harmful. We find that we cannot quote from this letter, because it is written in an inadmissibly offensive manner. But we are ready at any moment to show it to the editors of *Literaturnaya Gazeta*.

We recognize the justice of *Literaturnaya Gazeta*'s demand that readers' mail should be treated objectively and some idea should be given of the range of opinion expressed by readers, if only by indicating the *number* of letters supporting either side in a controversy. *Novy Mir* proposes to follow this practice in future in its "Readers' Forum." It is much to be desired that *Literaturnaya Gazeta* do likewise.

EDITORIAL BOARD OF *Novy Mir*